To Fred

Diffusing Power

With every
good wish,
in comradeship,
Michael Meacher

Diffusing Power

The Key to Socialist Revival

Michael Meacher

Pluto Press

London

First published in 1992 by Pluto Press
345 Archway Road, London N6 5AA

British Library Cataloguing in Publication Data
A catalogue record for this book is available from
the British Library.

ISBN 0 7453 0692 6   hb
ISBN 0 7453 0693 4   pb

Typeset from author's discs by Archetype.
Printed in Finland by WSOY.

Contents

Foreword

Can Labour ever win? After Labour's fourth election defeat in April 1992, the pessimists are in full cry, though they vary in their explanations. Tax, Tory tabloid vitriol, the premature triumphalism of the Sheffield rally, distrust of the leadership – all may have played a part. But the fundamental reasons go deeper than these superficial causes. One has to ask why, amid the worst recession for 60 years and with the most desultory Tory campaigning performance in living memory, Labour never got beyond a 1–2 point poll lead. The fact is, the right can win by claiming to manage the status quo; the left can only win by inspiring people with a clear and strong vision of a different and better society.

Labour has lost its old ideology and not yet found its new inspiration. I can still quite clearly remember a senior member of Labour's National Executive Committee saying in frustration and anguish some two years ago: 'Well, what *does* the left now really stand for?' Flummoxed for other than a glib rhetorical answer, it made me search long and hard for a response that was both politically powerful and intellectually credible. This book is the outcome.

Everywhere, it seemed, orthodox socialism was in retreat. Not only with the fall of the Berlin Wall and the implosion of the command economies throughout the Eastern bloc, but the bandwagon for the right appeared unstoppable both in the Anglo-Saxon countries of the USA and UK, in the Southern world of Latin America and Africa, and even in the Northern socialist enclave of Scandinavia. Yet with countless others I did not believe, and never will believe, that the great historical project of human emancipation – socialism – was over.

The socialist agenda, it seemed to me, was as compelling and urgent as ever. But after the huge upheavals in the political and economic climate of the 1970–80s, the left, unlike the right, had not reinterpreted its core message in forms and structures that made sense in the transformed landscape of what many felt was a new era. The left could no longer survive, especially with young voters, as the proponent of a benevolent and bureaucratic Welfare State, hostile to individual freedom. Nor could it take refuge in the old nostrums of nationalisation or import controls which seemed Canute-like to be vainly resisting a more interdependent economic order. Even less would it satisfy to fall back on oppositionism: simply being against the European Community, against nuclear weapons, against multi-national corporations.

What is the left *for*? What *positively* did socialism now stand for? One answer which many social democratic parties throughout the West have sought to propound is a more fully rationalised and meritocratic social order based on the 'mixed economy' and back-up welfare provision. But whatever else, that is not socialism. It is rather a modernised and humanised form of state capitalism. Another answer has been to assert the goal of a materialistic utopia, whilst claiming a superior collectivist means to achieve it. But that is to accept the capitalist fallacy that man has no soul, and to ignore that the essential aims of socialism are justice and liberty.

There is nothing debasing in rethinking a political philosophy. Karl Marx wrote *Das Kapital* in the London of the 1850s, but it is safe to assume that if he returned to the London of a century and a half later, he would write a completely different book, since the capitalist economy he was describing has changed out of all recognition. Indeed it is the duty of every new generation of socialists not to venerate the great works of the past, but to reassess and re-present their historic vision in a manner that is relevant and meaningful to the actual modern world of their contemporaries.

This is one contribution to that task. It recognises the force of the micro-chip-driven change to a decentralised economy, and of the shift from the postwar one-third affluent/two-thirds poor society of community values to the two-thirds affluent/one-third poor society of aspiring individualism today. It embraces power to the individual to the maximum feasible extent. But it is not about mere top-down democratisation or empowerment. It is about an internal seizure of power, or more precisely, a deliberate appropriation of power from the inside.

It insists too that widened power and choice be used for community and altruistic ends. For socialism in the last analysis is about people banding together in support of a common good beyond themselves. If then extending power to people to gain control over their own lives is a necessary condition of socialism, winning people to use that enhanced power for social and community ends greater than themselves is its sufficient condition. How it should be done in the new economic and political conditions of today's world is the theme, the Big Idea, of this book.

Abbreviations

ACAS	Advisory, Conciliation and Arbitration Service
ACPO	Association of Chief Police Officers
BT	British Telecom
CFC	Chloro-fluorocarbons
CGT	Capital Gains Tax
CND	Campaign for Nuclear Disarmament
COHSE	Confederation of Health Service Employees
CPVE	Certificate of Pre-Vocational Education
DSS	Department of Social Security
ECOFIN	Economic and Financial Council of Ministers
EMS	European Monetary System
EMU	Economic and Monetary Union
ERM	Exchange Rate Mechanism
ESOP	Employee Share Ownership Schemes
ET	Employment Training
G7	Group of Seven
GCHQ	Government Communications Headquarters
GDP	Gross Domestic Product
GLC	Greater London Council
GLEB	Greater London Enterprise Board
GNP	Gross National Product
IMF	International Monetary Fund
IT	Information Technology
LDC	Less Developed Countries
LEA	Local Education Authority
MSC	Manpower Services Commission
NEC	National Executive Committee
NHS	National Health Service

NUM	National Union of Mineworkers
OECD	Organisation for Economic Co-operation and Development
OPA	Open Press Authority
OPEC	Organisation of Petroleum Exporting Countries
PLP	Parliamentary Labour Party
PR	Proportional Representation
PSBR	Public Sector Borrowing Requirement
R&D	Research and Development
RUC	Royal Ulster Constabulary
TEC	Training and Enterprise Council
TGWU	Transport and General Workers Union
TVEI	Technological and Vocational Initiative
UDA	Ulster Defence Association
UGC	University Grants Committee
UNCTAD	United Nations Conference on Trade and Development
YTS	Youth Training Scheme

1

Conservatism Rampant: the Market Uber Alles

The fourth successive election defeat for the Labour Party in April 1992 cast the left into disarray. It was not only that Labour, after strenuously disciplined campaigning over the previous two years, still ended up with a lower proportion of the vote than in 1935. It was much more that the prospect of 18 years out of power presented the left with an identity crisis. Did it still have a role in contemporary Britain?

There has never been a greater need on the left for a clear statement of exactly what its alternative is. There can be no harking back to the hackneyed nostrums of a past age. The left must face up to the demands of the radically changed political, social and economic landscape of the 1990s, for the left cannot rest on a static or utopian aspiration to a world as one would like it to be. If it is going to mobilise mass support, it must have a dynamic about it, a capacity to unlock new forces now pent up, an inspiration to arouse new political excitements. A project of such magnitude requires the contribution of a thousand hands. This book seeks to point the direction.

The source of the left's identity crisis is set by what has been called the Thatcherite revolution. In fact there were three fundamental facets underlying her ascendancy in the 1980s – the economic, the ideological and the underpinning of power dominance. At least to the high point following her third election victory in 1987, all three were successfully intertwined. What the left requires is a radical project with the same internal coherence and inspirational drive. For that reason the starting point must be an examination of the Thatcherite model in each of its modes since

1

it remains the overriding ethos when her successor has supplied no ideological distinctiveness to replace it.

The Economic Record and Rising Living Standards

At least until the summer of 1988 Thatcher and Lawson were widely credited with bringing about an economic miracle. Sustained improvements in supply-side productivity were attributed to privatisation, de-regulation of markets, tight control of public expenditure and anti-trade union laws trimming back labour power. As a result, it was thought, a seven-year burst of rising economic growth 1982–89 saw inflation cut back to a low of 3 per cent a year, productivity rising faster than in any other of the seven biggest industrial nations except Japan, a budget surplus reaching £15 billion a year or more, and the living standards of the average-paid worker soaring over the decade to 1989 by a stunning 29 per cent. It seemed impressive enough at the time to have broken the century-old cycle of British economic decline.

The rebirth of competitive capitalism however turned into a summer mirage. What was proclaimed as a supply-side miracle turned out to be a straightforward expansion of demand, led by consumption, on exactly the old model and with exactly the same bad results in stop-go-stop that bedevilled the economy from the 1950 to the 1970s.

In the over-rigid monetarism of the Thatcher government's first two years, total output of the British economy fell by 5 per cent, a fifth of manufacturing industry was bankrupted, manufacturing investment fell by nearly 30 per cent and unemployment almost trebled to over 3 million. Then, after winning the 1979 election on a programme of tight money, the government undertook the biggest reflationary U-turn of all time. After obstinately refusing to reflate the economy out of slump by public expenditure, they reflated it on an even bigger scale by private credit.

By de-regulating the financial markets and removing controls on bank lending, the government unleashed the credit boom which soon grew at an astronomic pace. In the years 1981–4 the money supply (which they had sworn to limit) was jacked up no less than 50 per cent, twice as fast as the government's official target. In the next four years it was pushed up further by 20 per cent a year, just about doubling again in the process.

The idea of a supply-side miracle (there have been improvements, though generally modest) built on tight control of demand, which was supposed to be the foundation of the Thatcherite economic revolution, turned out therefore to be a gigantic con-trick. It was based instead on an all-too-conventional expansion of demand, only this time of consumer debt rather than public expenditure. In the three years 1986–8 people's incomes from work grew by 3 per cent a year, but their spending rose by double that. The difference was made up by bank borrowing: consumer debt rose in real terms by a huge 12 per cent a year. Non-mortgage borrowing from the banks by individual customers rose from £14 billion in 1983 to no less than £34 billion in early 1989.

With the level of demand escalating out of control far beyond the 3–4 per cent growth rate of the economy, the result was the ballooning trade deficit, running in 1989 at an unprecedented £20 billion a year (at nearly 4 per cent of gross domestic product, bigger proportionately than for the US). It also led to a tripling in the rate of inflation to 10.9 per cent in 1990, double the EEC average. So much for the Grantham housewife's homily that nations like families should 'always live within their means'.

For these reasons the first pillar of the Thatcherite project – a sustained economic recovery – fell apart and led ultimately to her downfall. Even the huge budget surplus of £15 billion in 1988–9, seen at the time as the seal of her success, represented anything but a strong economy. It reflected rather proceeds from privatisation (£7 billion in 1989), cutting the rise in pensions in line only with prices and not earnings as in the 1970s (a saving to the exchequer of £5 billion in 1989 alone and of £24 billion in total over the previous decade), and North Sea oil revenues (now falling, but still £3 billion in 1989). Public investment, which lays the foundation for the nation's quality of life, was massively cut back from 6 per cent of gross domestic product in the early 1970s to less than 2 per cent in the 1980s, with consequences of dilapidation in our housing, schools, health service and roads that everyone can see: private affluence for the few, public squalor for all, with a vengeance.

The Ideological War

The second leg of the Thatcherite tripod lay in the ideological drive. She did not simply follow the market as a guiding mechanism; she consistently and aggressively deployed it as an ideological weapon to assert her fundamental values. Those ideas have a compelling simplicity about them. They are that the criteria of the market should prevail not only in the economy, but throughout the social and political life of the nation generally; that therefore privatisation and rolling back the frontiers of the state should be pushed to the furthest feasible degree; and that as a consequence of the first two, individual responsibility should be paramount. Such a paean to pure individualism reached its climax in her assertion that 'there is no such thing as society.'

Thatcher did not originate these ideas, despite the whole philosophy behind them being attributed to her. What she did rather was build on pre-existing trends in Britain and major changes already apparent in other Western capitalist countries, and crystallise them in a clear, central theory. A shift towards a more monetarist approach in treasury budgeting had already occurred in 1976, and the public service ethos across a whole range of social and public services was already being steadily eroded through the 1950s to 1970s. Furthermore, the old post-war growth pattern based on a balanced expansion of mass production and mass consumption within national economies came to an end in the early 1970s. A new mode of growth emerged based on more flexible and specialised production, more closely tailored to individual consumer need, within an internationally more open and competitive economy. The shift was apparent throughout the Western economies, not just in Britain. What Thatcher did, skilfully and earlier than most, was identify these trends and appropriate them to her own highly political ends.

Those ends have been the creation of a 'popular capitalism' to overturn the social democratic consensus of the 1950s and 1960s. This programme was systematically pursued in each main arena – in the economy, in society and the organisation of services, and in the running of the state and civil order. Together they implied a major restructuring of British society, to be achieved only through the creative destruction of old institutions and social forces.

The Market as the Measure of All Things

In the economic sphere, the elevation of market forces as the untrammelled arbiter has been unrelenting. In place of incomes policies, subsidies to lame ducks and corporatist bargaining, the Thatcher governments stressed the dynamising effects of flexibility, inequality and competition. The chosen instruments to bring this about were privatisation, de-regulation (the removal of all controls over the operation of unfettered markets) and an emphasis on commercial criteria in government decision-making and public services.

As the transition to a fully open international economy gathered pace, Thatcherite economics gave pride of place to Britain's position as the principal site for international (for which read 'foreign') financial institutions. Through the abolition of exchange controls (which over the decade led to the transfer of a gigantic £140 billion of securities overseas), the de-regulation of financial services and favourable tax treatment, the City has been placed in a dominant position over manufacturing. It has also benefited greatly from the continuing series of huge privatisation issues and from the successive reductions in the public sector.

This programme of removing all constraints on capital has been matched by the removal of all protections from labour. A run of six anti-trade union laws has severely hamstrung labour's capacity to resist or negotiate on major structural changes in the workplace, almost wholly to its disadvantage. Less concerned with re-skilling the labour force than maximising the flexibility of wages, hours and working conditions, the Tory governments with open partisanship bent the law overwhelmingly in favour of the employer. In addition, the whole of the lower half of the labour market has been restructured around a two-nations market solution: a central core of full-time, well-paid, high-skilled workers is now supplemented by a growing under-class, now a third of the entire labour force, of part-time, poorly paid, low-skilled, increasingly casualised workers with little or no security.

In the social sphere, Thatcher's ideology was directed at supplanting the social democratic welfare state by a neo-liberal minimum social security state. The principles of the post-war social settlement – based on citizens' rights, universal benefits and a rising standard of financial or material provision for all, including the poorest – was abandoned in favour of a social regime that was discretionary, means-tested and minimalist.

Popular capitalism was to substitute for the 'granny state'. House-owning, pension-owning, share-owning and private medical insurance were subsidised through tax reliefs and large discounts, and were intended to replace council housing, adequate state pensions, proper income support and high-quality health services available to all as of right. Where individuals and families could not (or would not) make adequate private provision, social policy was scaled down to a basic no-frills state system, increasingly subject to rationing by queueing or based on revolving, cash-limited 'social funds' so that the poor paid for themselves.

This reorganisation of the welfare state did not lead to much overall reduction in public spending on welfare – indeed probably the reverse when the soaring costs of mass unemployment and the huge increase in tax reliefs are taken into account. However, its effects on life styles, social differences and political attitudes have been considerable. How far these innovations have contributed to the relief (or worsening) of poverty and deprivation was clearly irrelevant to the Thatcher government. Its purpose was to manage the *political* repercussions of the transition from mass-production national economies to the flexible specialisation of the open world economy, and not with the real conditions in which the submerged third of the population live. If they can be ignored as social junk rather than requiring careful handling as social dynamite, so much the better. The massaging of the unemployment figures was symptomatic of this general strategy.

The third element in Thatcher's ideological strategy was not only governmental disengagement from the economic scene to let the market prevail unfettered, but the tackling of the social, political and cultural factors that obstructed the transition to the open market system. That has meant the intensification of state control over important areas of social and economic life and the regular curtailment of institutions of political democracy.

Throughout the decade power was increasingly concentrated in the executive branch of government, while the parliamentary legislature was repeatedly marginalised as a rubber-stamp. The opponents of pure market ideology, most notably the trade unions, the Labour Party and local government, were repeatedly assailed as the 'enemy within', while a combination of legislative and administrative measures was continually deployed to undermine their power and even their existence. Thatcher's pledge to eliminate socialism for ever was the keynote symbol for policies to disorganise potential opposition.

The Market at Bay

How successful was this ideological assault? It is undeniable that Thatcher's obsession with markets profoundly shook up many areas of economic and public life too long dormant. There can be no doubting too the benefits of markets, as Thatcher so often proclaimed, in terms of their efficiency, the freedom of choice they offer to consumers and their circumvention of officialdom.

It is also clear that repudiation of markets altogether by some of Thatcher's opponents is wholly misplaced. It cannot be emphasised too strongly that there can be no socialist (or any other) objection to the technical character of market transactions as such, that is a forum where willing sellers of goods or services exchange with willing buyers. It is the specific nature of *capitalist* markets, which polarise enormous inequalities in purchasing capacity and concentrate enormous economic power narrowly in a few hands, that is objected to.

Market systems in fact suffer from a range of imperfections of different kinds – pragmatic drawbacks, economic, social and environmental, and value deficiencies perhaps best described as metaphysical. All of these have to be closely weighed against claims of superior efficiency.

Economically, market economies generate damaging consequences in the form of what are called 'externalities', that is benefits or more often losses affecting those not directly involved. Thus polluters are only concerned that their activities make a profit, not that they may damage or poison the environment. Because companies are committed only to their own internal accounting and not to potential wider social costs, their activities are not necessarily consistent with the general public good.

Markets, even within their own parameters, are readily destabilised and adjust in a flawed manner. Whether in exchange rates or share prices, the market regularly tends to overshoot. The sharp upward revaluation of sterling from $1.60 to $2.45, and then down again to $1.05, all within a five-year period to 1985, was not only hugely damaging to export firms, but also grossly exceeded any oscillations in the real economy.

Markets also tend to extremes by over-rewarding success and over-punishing failure. For similar reasons they tend too towards monopoly where large and successful firms over-dominate while small competitors can easily be squeezed out. De-regulation, the withdrawal of all controls over market operations, so far from from releasing dynamic and increasing efficiency, can seriously backfire. Thus the de-regulation of financial markets in the early 1980s unleashed the enormous credit boom that pushed both inflation and the trade deficit out of control in 1989 and forced the recession in 1990–2 before stability could be restored.

But the flagship of Thatcher's marketeering remained the privatisation programme. Her fanatical antagonism to nationalisation prompted the removal from public ownership of almost the entire stock of public sector companies and industries, even carrying ideological fervour to the extreme of privatising basic public utilities like electricity, gas and water. Yet there has been little evidence of any sustained improvement in market criteria such as efficiency or profits post-privatisation over and above what would anyway have happened in the bull market of 1983–9. In the case of the bigger and more important industries, the exercise has been little more than turning a public monopoly into a private one. The costs on the other hand have been considerable: billions of pounds were given to the City for arranging the sales and further billions were scattered in free giveaway or under-priced shares (one might surmise that such enormous bribes did not exactly suggest a public vote of confidence in the so-called 'popular capitalism'). The main item that has shown an unmistakable increase has been the level of boardroom salaries once directors were safely ensconced in the private sector.

The social consequences of Thatcher's market ideology have been the polarisation of society, the systematic rundown of public services, and the re-emergence of poverty on a significant scale. The market always produces inequality and Thatcher's extreme market policies have produced extreme inequality. A tiny elite of super-rich has been spawned at the same time as poverty, according to official measures, now afflicts up to a fifth of the population.

In the name of the market too, social rights and benefits for women, young people, pensioners, the unemployed and employees at work have all been severely curtailed. Reduced health and safety protection at work, loss of protection against unfair dismissal for part-time workers, constant erosion of workers' rights to redress in industrial disputes, and endless chipping away at benefit entitlements for every category of claimant in need have all been carried through to maximise flexibility for capital and to enforce the work ethic irrespective of need. Even the Euro Social Charter, unanimously endorsed by Britain's eleven EEC partners in 1989 as a charter of workers' social rights to balance the intensified capitalism of the 1992 Single Market, was repudiated uniquely by Thatcher in the name of the market.

At a deeper level Thatcherism represented the triumph of the tinsel society. By grossly under-investing in the seed-corn of the nation's future – training, R&D, social infrastructure and regional balance – and by cream-skimming the immediate gains in the form of tax hand-outs, free shares and housing capital discounts, the market philosophy took the 'Me, Now' society to new heights. Individualism degenerated into selfishness, self-reliance into indifference about others and get-rich-quick greed was elevated into a national totem – the tombola economy with a vengeance.

The old class barriers of noblesse oblige have wilted under assault from the hard-nosed purveyors of the new spiv capitalism. But a new class system has been generated, built more consciously on money, American-style. Ostentatious yuppie consumption – a Porsche, exotic holidays, a luxury penthouse in dockland, the party-going round – became the hallmark of success in ultra-materialistic market Britain.

The environment too has been forced to succumb to the dictates of the market. Because it represents a social cost and not a source of profit, environmental regulation has been grossly neglected. Any strategy for managing the rising quantities of toxic, hazardous and chemical wastes has been ignored. Some 11 million people are forced to drink water below minimum EEC quality standards, especially with excessive nitrate levels, because extensive use of chemical fertilisers for agriculture, which gradually seep into and poison the water supply, is highly profitable. Britain now has the dirtiest beaches in Europe and remains the worst offender for dumping in the North Sea because it is cheaper to dispose of untreated sewage sludge and other waste materials in that way. Also the Thatcher governments repeatedly dragged their feet over acid rain, though Britain remains the single biggest emitter of sulphur dioxide in Europe, because profitable industry took priority over preserving the environment.

In all these ways therefore Thatcher's ideological championing of the market may have invigorated the country's entrepreneurial drive, but it did so at enormous social cost, often gratuitously so. What she possessed in single-mindedness, she lacked in sense of balance. The case against her is not that her emphasis on market economics should be repudiated, but that she inflated her insistence on its dominance out of all proportion to the other desirable goals of a civilised society. Moreover the fact that she did so was no accident. For her adherence to the market was not only as an economic loadstone, but much more as a weapon for the pursuit of the sectional interests she politically represented. It is that inter-twining of the economic and the ideological which the left, while rejecting the content of the Thatcherite project, must emulate if it is to secure comparable authority.

The Drive for Dominance

While the market may be the standard-bearer, the whole point of Thatcherism as a form of politics was to construct a new social bloc to unite the political forces required to carry through radical change in the interests of the hard-line right and their economic backers. A social bloc is by definition not homogeneous. It does not consist of one whole class or even part of one class. It has to be welded together out of groups which are very different in their material interests and social positions.

Thatcher's achievement was to construct such a social bloc around the theme of what Stuart Hall has termed 'authoritarian populism'. She used this to condense a wide range of popular discontents with the post-war political and economic order and to mobilise them around dictatorial right-wing solutions to the central predicaments facing the country. Like so much else, this device was not invented by Thatcher, but rather appropriated to her use from strong political trends already implicit before her rise to power.

As the post-war settlement gradually broke down in the 1950s and 1960s amid successive balance of payments crises signalling Britain's relative economic decline, the governing strategy turned to corporatism. This reflected a centralised contract between government, business and labour to establish national controls over the 'anarchy' of the market in the name of order, unity and nationalism. When this too gradually disintegrated in the 1970s amid dangerously rising levels of international inflation, the growing public sense of the ungovernability of Britain paved the way for a much tougher social discipline and a more coercive exercise of state power at the expense of consensus. Thatcherism thus neatly matched the political demand at the end of the 1970s for a more disciplined state with the economic requirement increasingly pressing at the same time for a switch to a more flexible international capitalism.

Thatcher deployed her authoritarian populism in five main ways. She ruthlessly used state patronage to advance those of her own factional tendency not only in the state machine but throughout the serried ranks of the establishment. Her insistent query 'Is he one of us?' became a byword of partisanship in appointments to the great offices of state. Second, she was at pains to cultivate a special relationship with the police and security services, the main agents of state control, and ready to put them to paramilitary use when required in the interests of her social bloc (for example in the miners' strike). Third, she deliberately and systematically eliminated dissent, as her string of victims testifies (Ponting, GCHQ, the BBC, Spycatcher, the Tory 'Wets', the Greenham Common women, and many others) – symbols of a personal absolutism rather than a political democracy. Fourth, she sought not merely to wrongfoot her political opposition, but actually to destroy it (for example the GLC, trade unions and her 'mission to eliminate socialism'). And fifth, and most important of all, she inserted everywhere cadres for Thatcherism as her shock troops on the ground (entrepreneurs to run everything, private urban development corporations to replace local authorities, general managers to introduce the market into the NHS).

But these strong-arm tactics of the revolutionary leader to carry through a transformation of society in depth were always accompanied by Thatcher's projection of her ideology to clothe such tactics with legitimacy. The frontal attack on Labour was justified by the 'loony left' label which mischievously concocted in a single image high rates, political extremism and a racist/sexist backlash. For privatisation she constructed an image of the new share-owning working class and sought to expand the bloc symbolically round the image of 'choice'. For health and education she projected the image of quicker service via private health and a better chance for kids in a de-regulated education system with 'fast lane' schools and inner-city technology colleges. And in an over-bureaucratised, over-regulated, under-resourced society her slogan 'power to the people' carried a resonance far beyond her traditional bailiwick.

Thatcher's aggressive pursuit of authoritarian populism certainly played an important role in demoralising opposition to what would otherwise have been seen as her unacceptable extremism. The lessons for the left are that a clearly designed project around a forceful and commanding theme is now essential to build and maintain political dominance as a counterpoise to the right. Yet even understanding of the need for such a leadership strategy, with its own controlling agenda and facilitating ideology, is still lacking on the left.

That is not to say however that Thatcher's themes or methods should be copied. Indeed in terms of their corruption, cynicism and anti-democratic leanings they should be roundly condemned. Resentment became widespread at the whole idea of elective dictatorship and over-mighty government, and the fundamental British doctrine of the separation of powers was clearly seen to be under threat. Civil liberties have been under attack before, but over the decade of the 1980s they were steamrollered in the manner of an East European state. The acquiescence in the need for disciplined order in 1979 turned full circle by 1989 into rising indignation against autocracy.

For all that, the left ignores the positive achievements and lessons of Thatcherism at their peril. Thatcher advanced the techniques of political struggle on to a qualitatively new plane. That is not to be derided or abused. It must be matched if another power is to rise up, if another dominant bloc is to emerge, to overcome hers which even after her demise remains largely in place.

2

A Power-sharing Economy

It is no accident that Thatcher was such a strong advocate of market capitalism. For it is anything but the impersonal and objective system dedicated to efficiency that hordes of Western economists assure us it is. It is in fact a strongly value-loaded system riddled with predispositions that heavily colour the outcomes. It is above all a power system.

Free markets favour the strong and penalise the weak. While they are supposed in theory to contain an in-built mechanism for self-correction of excessive economic disequilibrium, in power terms they have the opposite effect. The acquisition of a measure of personal or corporate economic power serves only to accelerate the acquisition of more, while those possessing little or no power in the market find their position weakened further. For those, like Thatcher, who want a society dominated by an economic elite, a market ideology offers a perfect vehicle.

Moreover market systems shape more than the distribution of income and wealth in a characteristically unequal direction. The great institutions of state – big business, City finance, the media, the civil service and the government machine, the legal system, and major public services – all reach an accommodation with the market and are infected with its ethos. None is to be viewed strictly as the objective or dispassionate purveyor of a key public function. All are power systems within their own right and given the extreme inequality of the market environment within which they co-exist, that power is heavily concentrated at the top. Indeed it is the inter-relationships between those who hold the command positions within these hierarchies that determine the power structure in contemporary Britain. They are not a ruling class in the Marxist sense since they are a disparate group and not united around the same position vis-a-vis the productive system. But together they form the dominant power bloc that controls Britain.

The central task of left-wing politics is to tackle this ruling bloc with the same radical and persistent determination that Thatcher displayed towards *her* political opponents. Only then does fundamental reform become seriously possible. This book is therefore designed to lay out a framework as to how this might be done. This present chapter sets out an ideology to mobilise the forces and ideas to overturn the grip on public consciousness exerted by the right since the early 1980s.

Power for All, Not Just the Few

Marx saw the key to the transformation of capitalist society in the seizure by the working class of the ownership of the means of production, distribution and exchange. It is an analysis, penetrating when it was made in the early nineteenth century, that has served for too long as an excuse to avoid new creative thinking to match socialist aspirations in a world changed out of all recognition in the last 150 years. Indeed it can be safely assumed that Marx, if he were alive today, would produce a wholly different prescription to counter the completely different landscape of capitalism in the late twentieth century. For he himself would be the first to appreciate – even if his latter-day zealous disciples are not – that he over-stated the importance of ownership as opposed to control, under-stated the role and power of trade unions, assumed (wrongly) the growing and cataclysmic 'immiseration of the proletariat' and (not surprisingly) did not anticipate the fundamental changes of modern technology.

Yet where the Marxist model still points the way is in identifying the locus of power as the key criterion distinguishing a capitalist from a socialist society, and in insisting that a central facet of socialism lies in mobilising the mass of the people to throw off or abolish the source of the power used by a privileged minority to exploit the majority. Hence the *form* of Marx's analysis was right, but the *nature* of the capitalist power he sought to counter has profoundly changed. Power in contemporary society is not now uniquely, or even primarily, vested in industrial ownership. It is located rather in the ranks of senior management in big business, in the top levels of the civil service in an increasingly complex and regulated society, in the directors of the big financial companies in the City of London, in the controllers of the media and information networks in a technical society where information is power, and in top officials in the large public bureaucracies.

Neither Markets nor Statism

How is the left to deal with this concentration of power which ensconces privilege and opportunity in the hands of right-wing elites? The post-war answer was to wrest the 'commanding heights' of the economy from their grasp and vest them instead under public control. The results however, while full of promise in the 1940s, lost their shine over the next 30 years.

Monopoly industries and large-size firms, while conferring technical economies of scale, were plagued by over-centralised decision-making and remoteness which lowered labour morale. The objective of planning in the public interest proved scarcely easier to achieve under public than private ownership because ministers held to the Morrisonian concept of the independent public board. The dangers of monopoly in inhibiting choice of goods and suppliers loomed larger. Savings were not brought under public control because the boards did not build up surpluses. Whitehall interference, especially Tory ministers holding down prices, undermined efficiency and generated deficits and loss of morale. And as mass production capitalism gave way to flexible specialisation, nationalised industries came to be seen in many Western countries like stranded whales beached after their heyday of the 1930s to the 1970s.

Nor did nationalised industries succeed much better, partly due to the timidity of Labour governments, in their social objectives. Ministers continued to pick top managers from the private sector who were steeped in the ethos far more of capitalist markets than of socialist community (which inspired the quip that nationalisation plus Lord Robens does not equal socialism). The consumer interest was never effectively represented. And the goal of public service, or the idea of community benefit as opposed to market profitability, was never translated into practical policy: a social interest criterion of viability was never developed to override pure commercial market principles.

But if public ownership, at least in the traditional form associated with statism and monolithic bureaucracy, does not give that access to power for the wider mass of the people that socialists earlier hoped, neither does the Thatcherite model of the market. The parade of share offers and discounts as the avenue to choice and consumer power is more fantasy than real. Giving 'Syd' £200 of privatised British Gas shares may be a wonderful something-for-nothing bribe, but it does not increase consumer rights over pricing, bill queries, cut-offs or quality of service. Choice in a capitalist market is about being the passive recipient of this or that material thing. It is not about empowering people to live their own lives in the fullest sense in their own way.

Right-wing market formulae do not give access to, let alone control over, any of the big decisions that fundamentally determine the quality of people's lives. Decisions about what goods are produced and what services offered, who is hired or fired, and how much is invested for future work and where and in what form, are all taken by employers and holders of big capital. Employees do not have a say and nor do consumers who cannot choose what is not on offer. Do consumers feel the market offers them power to shape to their liking services like road and rail transport, the mass media, local repairs and maintenance, or adult education; or are new mechanisms needed to provide effective redress for complaints? In the all-important area of enforcing rights in a free society, the market offers only extremely unequal access to the law. Nor does it offer any effective means to counter abuse of power by the police, newspaper owners, local authority planners, schools or teachers, the health authority or doctors, and companies or their managers.

The State as Enabler

So neither a remote, bureaucratic, centralised state nor an unfettered Thatcherite market system can release the power and opportunities for individuals to gain real control over their environment so as to develop their full potential as they choose. But there is a third and better way.

Instead of the post-war socialist aspiration for the state to *supersede* market forces, which was not only over-ambitious but would raise as many problems as it resolved, the state should take the role of catalyst. Instead of seeking to be the universal provider, it should act, in different contexts, as regulator, advocate, enabler or protector.

It is linking the state to the cause of socialist individualism. No doubt for some for whom socialism is defined exclusively as state control over the commanding heights of the economy, this expression may seem a contradiction in terms. But that is to ignore that state versus markets is not so much an irreconcilable antithesis as a continuum where different trade-offs are possible. On the one side are the fundamentalist statists who pioneered the inflexible and bureaucratic 1940s nationalisations. On the other are the fundamentalist marketeers who currently champion untrammelled Thatcherite self-interest and want to roll back the state endlessly. In between are the advocates, on the one hand, of a much more flexible state regulation, and on the other of a much more constrained market system. Either of the two latter project a role for the state that is less heavy-handed, more innovative, more imaginative and indeed more of a stimulant if not directly entrepreneurial.

It means going a great deal beyond mere regulation in its present form. It means intervening not just to correct weaknesses in the operation of the market or to deal with externalities, but to shift economic activity towards explicit social objectives, in particular towards widening the spread of opportunities and power. Any number of examples might be cited. The state should play a major role in developing and monitoring employee democracy within companies and in extending arbitration for the resolution of internal disputes (not least to pre-empt strikes). It should propagate environmentalist goals by a mix of direct controls, tax incentives and subsidies. It should take the lead, through an independent panel of specialist consultants, in auditing management quality in both the public and private sectors.

As enabler the state should, again for illustration, provide for high-quality opportunity training for any who wish to switch careers in mid or later life into wholly new employment fields. It should award to disabled persons, young or elderly, grants according to their assessed degree of disability so that they can buy in services that they themselves choose. It should make available through a co-operative development agency technical, financial and managerial support for any group of employees who want to work under self-management auspices. Its financial support for physically, mentally or socially handicapped persons or for one-parent families should act not as an obstacle course precluding employment, but as a launching-pad to a job.

Nor should the state shrink from entrepreneurial initiatives, particularly where its special role makes it the most appropriate agent to perform a function. It should provide free legal aid and advice in inner city areas. It should offer a one-shop point in each local area for the comprehensive collection of house exchange data, as the best route to cheap and efficient conveyancing. It should provide both initial training and follow-through employment for a quality corps of contractors specialising in the whole range of household services and so on.

Empowering People

The facilitator role for the state is a key part of what should be the central theme of modern socialism. That theme is focused on the issue of power. Capitalist power lies in the concentration of control in a few hands of the main organisations that determine the future development of society. The essential characteristic of socialism by contrast is that control over people's lives is placed increasingly in their own hands.

Such a theme is not inconsistent with traditional formulations of socialism. These have centred round such ideas as the common ownership of the means of production, workers' control, welfare and equality, altruism and co-operative social relations, appropriating property incomes, and the brotherhood of man. These are all valid ideas in their own right, and there can be no question of reducing them to a single concept. Yet redistribution of power is at the heart of them all.

It is what common ownership, workers' control and the appropriation of property incomes were precisely designed to achieve. As regards welfare and equality (the Croslandite formula), it does not involve giving people things, whether money or services, which can entrench dependency, but it does mean finding ways to enable people themselves by their own means to overcome dependency or other limitations. Regarding co-operative social relations and the ideal of the brotherhood of man, it is certainly true that giving people greater control over their own lives is no guarantee of altruism. But it is precisely the social essence of socialism that demands that increasing power and opportunities must be balanced by enlarging responsibilities and obligations to others too.

Giving people power to gain control over their own lives has a myriad of applications. It offers a connecting thread which would direct reform into every corner of public life with the same thorough-going and comprehensive questioning, the same relentless drive, and the same highly charged political excitement and conviction as imbued some of the Thatcher years. And following the technique of that government of repeatedly returning to the same issue with fresh initiatives and additional acts of parliament, it means not one effort, not one statute, but constant and increasing pressure, using every supplementary device to hand, until a given objective can be progressively realised.

The sheer range of reform that would be unleashed needs to be illustrated. In education it means, not paying rhetorical lip-service to, but actually bringing about, an equal chance for individuals at the start of life. That in turn means breaking the inter-generational cycle of poverty and eroding the basis of a class-divided society. That has immense implications: closing the persistent health inequalities by class and region, substantially improving the poorer housing stock, attacking the debilitating physical and social dereliction of the inner cities, and significantly raising standards in both primary and secondary schools, especially for the lowest 40 per cent of the ability range.

Yet the implications go far wider than that. They affect the inheritance laws which grossly distort the pattern of opportunity, the public–private divide in education which is a licence geared to widen unequal chances in later life, the yawning chasm between academic training and vocational instruction at the tertiary stage during the crucially formative years of 16–19, and access to further education and higher training not only for the young, but throughout life. Education and training as the highway to opportunity are examined in Chapter 4.

Vesting control over people's lives in their own hands means fundamental reforms in the hierarchy of power within industry.

That is not just a matter of extending information, consultation and negotiation where at present they exist rather primitively. It means replacing unilateral managerial prerogative by jointly agreed control over key areas of decision-making. The mechanisms are discussed further in Chapter 10.

This theme also has big implications for people as consumers. It means providing effective redress against professional incompetence or negligence. It involves sharpening the principle of product liability against manufacturers, so that consumers damaged or cheated by defective or dangerous products have effective financial redress. It means overriding local bureaucracies in health, housing, education and social security. The means to do all this are explored in Chapter 8.

Giving people real control over their own lives also implies dramatic changes in the checks and balances against an over-mighty executive which is perhaps today the biggest threat to individual liberties. That requires a Freedom of Information Act and many other major reforms in our system of government: Chapter 6 goes into the details. It means securing regular access to the media for minority interests, as well as a right of reply for those abused by gross media bias: Chapter 7 explores the machinery.

Extending to the broad mass of the people the power and opportunity now reserved for the few must mean drastic reform of the present spread of incomes. Power in the market-place cannot be wielded by those crippled by poverty or excessively low pay. A minimum income threshold must be established which allows everyone to contribute creatively to society. Equally at the other end of the spectrum, if incentives are to be a motivating and unifying force, not a divisive one, top rewards should not be totally out of reach in some practical manner from the generality of workers. Far-reaching proposals to this end are made in Chapter 5.

Empowerment also means enlarging the area of creative rights. Industrial, social and welfare rights should not merely be a passive protection against the tyranny of the employer, the relevant authorities or the state. They should much rather be a device for individuals to overcome disadvantage so as actively to participate in whatever relevant forum they choose (Chapter 7). Similarly, widespread application of the latest technology can and should become a liberating force for all those marginalised in the labour market, whether by physical handicap, home circumstances or limited capital (Chapter 9). Information technology in particular can have almost limitless applications in making the world of work more rewarding and making decision-making more democratic (Chapter 10).

Above all, securing for people greater control over their own lives and future prospects has huge implications for regulation of the market. It makes full employment, or some close approximation to it, a central objective of policy. For nothing destroys a person's capacity to master their own destiny so much as extended unemployment. It requires active labour market policies to ease redeployment and to enforce employer responsibilities to retrain rather than make redundant wherever practicable. It means restructuring market power, both through tougher anti-monopoly action or divestment, regulation of takeovers so that the public interest and employees' consent is secured, and by assisting market entry for small businesses and new enterprise. These are explored in Chapter 12.

Empowering people to take control over their own lives goes to the heart of almost every area of economic activity, social welfare or civic regulation. It is an immensely exciting challenge. It not only opens up a fresh and much more attractive vista of socialism, it also offers the prospect of building an alliance across different classes and interests that can overcome the current ideological dominance of the radical right. It should now become the central theme for the left.

3

The Environment:
The Need to Change Direction

Whatever one's response to a socialist renewal, there are two fundamental areas where we cannot go on as we are. One concerns the ecological plunder of the planet and the other is, for want of a better phrase, the education system. This chapter and the next examines the implications of both these breakdowns and the proposed solutions in the light of the ideological struggle spelt out in Chapters 1 and 2.

Eco-despoliation has taken three main forms. One is threatened exhaustion of the basic raw materials of the planet as a result of the drive towards over-industrialisation. The second is the risk of global climatic destabilisation which could render a considerable portion of earth uninhabitable for complex forms of life. And the third is the peril to the quality of life of mankind and the steady poisoning of life-support systems themselves, from the vast and growing spread of pollutants.

The Finite Limits of Material Growth

One major argument challenging the capitalist scenario of endless material growth has been the eventual, and perhaps not very distant, limit to be imposed by depletion of the raw material base. In 1972 the Club of Rome published an MIT study which sought to show that 'if the present growth trends in world population, industrialisation, pollution, food production, and resource depletion continue unchanged, the limits to growth on this planet will be reached some time within the next 100 years.' Then in 1973 Paul Ehrlich's *The Population Bomb* predicted that a quarter of mankind would starve to death in the next decade.

It has not happened. Predictions of disaster that rely on

extrapolating past trends often turn out to be wrong. A year after *The Limits to Growth* was published, the oil price was quadrupled, and suddenly it was profitable to extract it from such intractable areas as the North Sea. A year after *The Population Bomb* appeared, the world's birth rate at last began to rise more slowly.

The eco-doomsters' forecasts have not been realised because the basic data of resource availability is very uncertain. Indeed, the fact that for many past decades each generation has ended its period of growth with larger amounts of 'proved' reserves of many resources than it started suggests that the size of our 'known' reserves is mainly determined by the effort we invest in looking for them. The huge Siberian sub-continent, for example, has barely been prospected, like the South American continent which may reveal as much totally unexpected wealth as did the rich Alaskan oil slope and the Libyan oil fields, both vast reservoirs discovered only in the last decade. Thus an 'optimistic' estimate of the availability of resources near the earth's surface may in reality not be 5 times present estimates, but 50 times. Moreover, potential reserves in the first mile of the earth's crust, which can be determined by geological sampling techniques, are many *thousand* times proved reserves (for example in the case of aluminium, more than 10 million times proved reserves).

This does not of course rescue the world from the problem of exponential growth per capita, but it does defer the day of reckoning for some generations. What it does mean is that, while metal ores are still very abundant, a slow upward trend in real costs is likely unless progress in extractive or consumption technology keeps pace with declining ore grades. The problem, at least for some time to come, is not so much one of sheer physical depletion as of mining and engineering technology and economic adjustment.

Yet whatever the timespan of complacency, there are still foreseeable limits within which the *exponential* growth of the world industrial mega-machine can be contained. Industrial expansion in the advanced nations is today growing at a rate of about 7 per cent a year – a rate that doubles total output every ten years. If therefore one looks ahead a period so short in historic time as 50 years, it is likely that industrial output, using existing techniques, will have increased at the exponential rate of five –

doubling in 10 years, quadrupling in 20 years, octupling in 30 years and so on. It is difficult to see the future availability of the whole range of necessary raw materials (or their substitutes) feeding this gargantuan process of exponential growth at 7 per cent per year compound for even a couple of centuries, let alone indefinitely.

Without apocalyptic predictions of world industrial growth suddenly coming to an abrupt halt or even (according to the MIT/Club of Rome forecasts) entering a prolonged and steep decline, the evidence does suggest that breakneck expansion with ever more sophisticated technology is not a sustainable model of development for the long-term future. It is true that human societies only change course fundamentally in the face of threats to their own internal dynamic, when confronted by forces or pressures that are absolutely irresistible. It is also clear that pressures have not built up to that point, yet. However, it would be a policy of craven neglect and irresponsibility for a government, even of a medium-sized power like Britain, to fail to press strenuously within international forums for the most authoritative technical and scientific evaluations to be made of the long-term consequences of the exponential growth of world industrial output.

If a broad consensus were gradually to emerge, it might begin to lay the official foundations for mobilising world opinion round a range of alternative models for economic and demographic development more consistent with planetary equilibrium. Such a prospect is dependent on intensified progress towards international co-operation, but equally such a project could make an important contribution to that end. It would have enormous implications not least for the power structures of the industrialised countries as well as for individual lifestyles. But it is not a matter that can be postponed very much longer, especially since it interlinks closely with two other issues of human survival.

The Risk of Global Climactic Destabilisation

The 1980s saw a big increase in public awareness – leading to the major success of the Green parties in the European elections in June 1989 – of ecological developments endangering the future of mankind. These include the greenhouse effect of global warming, the thinning of the ozone layer, the destruction of rain forests, the dumping of toxic waste and the effect of acid rain on lakes and trees.

Of these the most dangerous is global warming. It is caused by gases added to the atmosphere by unregulated market activities. The biggest contributor, responsible for some 40–45 per cent of the greenhouse effect, is carbon dioxide generated by burning fossil fuels, with carbon dioxide released by deforestation adding a further 10–15 per cent. Chlorofluorocarbons (CFCs) absorb solar heat very strongly and therefore contribute to the greenhouse effect, to the extent of about 20 per cent, as well as destroying the ozone layer. Other gases such as methane, brewed in rubbish tips, paddy fields and cows' stomachs, and nitrous oxides, given off by fertilisers, are responsible for the remaining 25 per cent of global warming.

Why does global warming matter? It is crucial because the climate that has allowed the growth of civilisation and agriculture is virtually certain to disappear. Small changes in the earth's temperature can have devastating effects. Already the earth has warmed by about half a degree centigrade over the last 100 years, and is likely to add another 1.5–4.5 degrees centigrade by the 2030s. The world has not been as much as 3 degrees warmer than today for some 2 million years, and if present trends continue, then less than a century from now the earth could be a massive 8.5 degrees warmer.

The most predictable result is rising sea levels, by between 8 inches and 4.5 feet by 2030. A 3 foot increase would flood such cities as New Orleans, Shanghai and Cairo, would cause 15 million people in Bangladesh to lose their homes and livelihoods, would ruin many of Asia's best rice-growing areas, and would swamp much of London, the Thames Estuary and many UK coastal towns, causing 15 million people in Britain and Ireland to lose their homes. Flooding however will probably do much less damage than changes to the world's winds, rains and ocean currents. The great grain-growing regions of the world, the American Mid-West (already in 1989 suffering the worst droughts since the dustbowls of the 1930s) and the Soviet grainlands, will become much drier, leading to sharp falls in crop yields.

Coping with the greenhouse effect is likely to prove enormously expensive. Building just one mile of sea wall can cost about £1 billion. Poor countries will not be able to afford to; rich countries might have to spend trillions of pounds. It has been calculated that coping with a 2.5 degree rise could soak up a crippling 3 per cent of the world's economic output each year.

There is one more depressing scientific consensus – that the warming up is somehow 'inevitable'. A study by the World Resources Institute in Washington recently showed that even a determined effort to fend off the greenhouse effect would 'only' postpone the warming expected by 2030 by some 30–60 years. Yet even that time would be worth buying – to breed drought-resistant crops, to fortify against the rising sea, to cut consumption of fossil fuels by at least a fifth within 15 years.

What should be done? First, and easiest, the production of CFCs should be stopped. They trap heat 10,000 times as well as carbon dioxide, they are mostly used in replaceable luxuries such as air conditioners and fast-food containers, they damage the protective ozone in the stratosphere, and they are made by big chemical companies which lack popular appeal. Stopping CFC production by 2000 would probably cut greenhouse warming, after a lag, by 15 per cent.

The biggest problem is carbon dioxide, which accounts for half of the greenhouse effect. Currently mankind is pumping over 5 billion tons of it into the atmosphere each year; at the present rate of increase, that will reach over 10 billion by 2010. Worse, it is estimated that the oceans, which at present absorb nearly half of the carbon dioxide released by burning fossil fuels, will only be taking about a quarter of man's (higher) output by 2030.

Reversing this process will require fundamental change that strikes at the heart of the political economy of both Third World and industrialised countries alike. First, the burning of the world's tropical forests must be stopped. At present, they are being destroyed at the rate of 100 acres every minute of the day – arguably the greatest biological disaster ever perpetrated by man and a threat to civilisation second only to thermonuclear war. Each year 100,000 square kilometres of tropical forest are lost – an area the size of England – and at this rate the world's virgin rain forests will have been annihilated within 50 years. Already each year the burning of these forests adds about 1.6 billion tons of carbon dioxide to the atmosphere. Moreover, that does double damage because tropical forests, when intact, soak up carbon dioxide by turning it into trees.

Stopping this catastrophic deforestation requires unprecedented international action. With Third World debt now standing at around $1 trillion and with the West now equally a victim of the consequences of destabilisation of the global climate, both sides now have a strong interest in debt-for-nature swaps. Chunks of debt could be written off in exchange for example for Brazil or Bolivia agreeing to preserve so many million acres of the Amazonian rainforest. All development projects that involve the destruction of forested areas, such as ranching, livestock rearing and plantations, must be stopped, and a worldwide programme of reafforestation made a priority. The West's development strategy, pressurising Third World countries to cash in their indispensable resources, including their forests, in exchange for superfluous items like armaments, domestic appliances, cars and packaged foods, must be fundamentally revised.

In addition, a series of major technical projects could significantly curb the carbon dioxide heat-trapping effect. It could be scrubbed out of the smoke in power station chimneys – more than 430 scrubbers have been fitted around the world, but none so far in Britain. A whole new industry could thrive on splitting methane into carbon fibre (as a competitor with metal) and hydrogen, to fuel cars. At present the world's 400 million cars contribute about 500 million tons of carbon dioxide to the atmosphere a year, yet cars burning hydrogen would make almost no carbon dioxide at all. And no doubt other ingenuities will be developed, as well as more obvious drives to expand energy conservation and hydro-electric power. Such improvements would in time pay for themselves; but they would cut carbon dioxide emissions by a mere 2 billion tons, about half the *increase* predicted for the period 1990–2010.

Clearly a more fundamental strategy is required. The centrepiece must be tough international political action to reduce significantly the global use of fossil fuels. The Toronto conference in June 1988 proposed a 20 per cent cut in carbon dioxide emissions by 2005, and a 50 per cent cut by 2025. Such an ambitious, though technically feasible and strictly necessary, target would impose enormous strains on industrial society. While the West imposed an 'atmospheric users' fee' on carbon, a programme for minimising the use of fossil fuels by developing countries, overwhelmingly responsible for future growth in energy use as they steadily industrialise, might require an international fund, paid for by the richer OECD nations, of some £200 billion over the next 15 years. However, in the post-1989 East–West detente ending the Cold War and thus paving the way for massive cuts in Western defence expenditure, such funding is clearly feasible, especially when the survival of the planet is at stake.

Around that core programme other radical policies should be fitted. An international accord should be sought to increase the area of the world's forests by at least 30 million acres a year for at least 20 years. A quantum increase in energy conservation, probably the most cost-effective way to slow global warming, should be achieved by radically sharpening incentives, for example through a vehicle tax geared to a car type's fuel efficiency, mandatory labelling of all appliances and domestic buildings to indicate their energy efficiency, and incentives to power-saving generating and heating systems. And new technology should be developed, in particular gas-fired electricity generation, which halves the carbon dioxide emissions of coal and costs only a fifth as much to build as a new coal-fired power plant.

The Pollution of Prosperity

The greatest ecological threats to the planet derive from global warming with associated floods, depletion of the ozone layer with associated cancer and disruption of the ocean food chains, and the acidification of forests, lakes, crops and buildings. The resources which have now become scarcest are unpolluted air, water and soil. The real limits to growth are the capacity of the environment to deal with waste in all its forms and the threat to resources which play no direct part in world commerce. These critical resources – the ozone layer, the carbon cycle, Amazonia – are treated as free goods when in fact they serve the most basic economic function of all, enabling people to survive.

Acid rain derives from the chemical pollutants, especially sulphur and nitrous oxides, spewed into the skies from power stations, heavy industrial plants and vehicle exhausts. As a result snow, rain, mists or fog become increasingly acidic and over time transmit a lethal degree of acidity to forests, lakes and soil. Already half of all German pine forests have been damaged, with two-thirds of all fir trees now diseased. The whole complex infrastructure of the aquatic environment has collapsed: 20,000 lakes in Sweden have lost their fish, just as once healthy, productive lakes in the US now produce nothing. With already 2–4 million square miles of our planet estimated by the UN environmental programme to be already affected, and with the estimated cost to EEC member states reckoned at 3–5 per cent of GNP, it is clear that it is not what it will cost us to carry out the necessary measures, but what it will cost us if we do not.

The ozone layer, which protects the earth from ultra-violet radiation, is becoming seriously depleted. It is expected to shrink by 1.5–5 per cent over the next few decades, and every 1 per cent decrease is expected to yield a 2 per cent increase in skin cancers, to retard the growth of crops, and to damage the undersea organisms which lie at the end of the food chain. Since CFCs are to blame, some 33 countries agreed in 1987 to freeze their consumption of these gases in 1990, to cut it by 20 per cent four years later, and to make a further 30 per cent cut eventually. That will still not stop chlorine levels in the stratosphere, which attack ozone, from reaching three times their present level by 2020. If we are really serious about getting rid of the ozone holes, a complete phase-out of CFCs is required.

Acid rain and destruction of the ozone layer are only the most striking illustrations of a much wider trend. Pollution is the usual by-product of economic activity and there is no global rubbish bin. The list is endless, whether for city dirt (with Milan and Shenyang heading the world league for sulphur dioxide pollution and New Delhi for grubby grains of airborne chemicals), contamination of water (for example half of Poland's water is too polluted even for industrial use and over four-fifths of its deep wells are polluted), acid fog (100 times more acidic than acid rain), the pollution of Antarctica, and the sharply rising emission of particulates by diesel vehicles. An American survey published in March 1989 found that 2.4 billion pounds of toxic chemicals, including many linked to birth defects and neurological defects, are pumped into the air every year over the US. In addition, there are the multiple exposures of the industrial radiation age from fallout, nuclear accidents, medical radiation, nuclear waste, radioactive consumer products, and the production of nuclear weapons and nuclear power.

It would be wrong however to pretend that these problems, given enough cash and technology, cannot be alleviated. London no longer suffers from the 'pea souper' fogs of 1952. The Tiber and Guadalquivir rivers carry twice as much oxygen as 15 years ago. Lead emissions in the US are only one-tenth the level of 1975. In the 1970s to early 1980s slower economic growth combined with tougher emission controls in the industrialised countries led to some striking reductions in air pollution. Several major countries, including the US, West Germany and Japan, cut emissions of sulphur dioxide.

These instances, while uncommon, belie the Green Parties' claim that the only antidote to worsening pollution is the stationary, growthless state. Moreover, a 'stationary' state – one in which industrial growth had ceased – would not necessarily be a society in ecological balance because it could still be polluting the environment. It would also impose intolerable costs on the developing world as well as enormous institutional strains on industrialised countries. Contrary to Green propaganda, it is not growth as such that is the mortal enemy, but pollution. Hence the Brundtland Report in 1987 on the world environment proposed the concept of 'sustainable development', within limits that ensure that the global environment is not destroyed. It is a concept that governments have paid lip service to, though none has faced up to its real implications.

Markets or Regulation?

How then to turn back the rising tide of pollution-generating growth before it swamps the delicate ecological balance of the planet? Such a question goes to the heart of the political economy not only of the next decade, but of the next century.

The foregoing analysis suggests four key principles that need to be observed. The first is that the market, so far from being the answer to ecological damage and pollution, is actually a major cause of the problem. For the main feature of mass-production markets is their dynamic of undifferentiated expansion: there are no 'good' or 'bad' categories of products, only those that make a profit and those that do not. There have been two market responses to this problem, yet neither is satisfactory.

One, recommended by Professor Barry Commoner in *The Closing Circle* in 1972, proposed an 'ecological impact inventory' so that a pollution price tag could be placed on each product. Such an inventory would then enable us to judge the relative social value of different processes and would guide us to return to natural products over synthetics. He also explored the multiplicative relationship of population, affluence and technology in the generation of pollution and concluded that the technology factor (that is the increased output of pollutants per unit of production resulting from new technologies since the 1940s) accounted for about 95 per cent of the massive rise in pollution in the US over the previous three decades. However, while the targeting of flawed technology offers an easy solution consistent with conventional market principles, it is simply not credible that population growth and increased affluence contributes as little as 5 per cent to environmental deterioration, or anywhere near it. Technology does need to be changed, but that by itself is only skirting the surface of the problem.

The other response to market destruction of the ecology has been the devising of meta-market solutions. If the market produces pollution, there is room for *more* growth for anti-pollution measures. If nuclear reactors produce unstorable waste, proceed to the next level of nuclear development with fast reactors that reprocess their own waste. If nuclear fission is too hazardous, move up the developmental scale to fusion. If natural products run out, invent artificial substitutes. There are no insoluble problems: a breakthrough a day keeps the crisis at bay.

What is wrong with this 'solution' is its total lack of perspective. Conventional water and air pollution is one thing; destabilisation within decades of biological conditions with narrow tolerances for human survival that have built up over geological eras is another. When plutonium, the material produced in every nuclear reactor, remains radioactive for 500,000 years, *no* degree of temporary prosperity can justify the accumulation of large amounts of highly toxic substances which nobody knows how to make safe and which remain an incalculable danger to the whole of creation for historical ages.

Market economics is blind to dimensional differences. It offers no value threshold to signal there is no point in material growth or higher living standards when the earth is contaminated by substances which cause malformations in our children or grandchildren. While economists mouth the words of ecologically sound growth, the market calculus of profit and loss offers no steer towards a non-violent, harmonious co-operation with nature or towards noiseless, low-energy, conservationist solutions. Quite the reverse – so much of mass production that is profitable for capitalists is ecologically damaging and self-defeating in its consumption of non-renewable resources, as well as inherently violent and stultifying for the human person. According to the laws of the market, advances in technology which increase profit are progress. Yet technological shifts towards greater size, speed and violence, when they overstep the laws of natural harmony, are the *opposite* of progress.

The second fundamental principle therefore is that observation of environmental limits cannot be left to the market. It requires clear and decisive regulation. At a minor level this can be achieved within the market system itself: make the polluter pay. Depletion taxes can be levied on the utilisation of resources according to their scarcity or non-renewability, and tax reliefs or grants given as incentives for conservation. But for more long-term lethal forms of pollution or ecological destruction, such market signals are wholly inadequate.

Devotees of the market like *The Economist* recommend green growth by such measures as 'introducing a sulphur dioxide tax or making power stations buy a permit to belch'. But auctioning a licence to pollute – where such pollution could overheat the planet, deplete the ozone layer or dump dangerously high levels of toxic waste – is like prohibiting murder, but then putting a licence to kill up for sale to be traded. Making companies buy permits to produce CFCs is the wrong approach. Either the gases are harmful to the planet, or they are not. If they are, the correct policy is to get their production stopped.

Indeed regulation is likely to be the order of the 1990s and beyond. Paradoxically, de-regulation, so far from unleashing the capitalist nirvana, is now increasingly seen as containing the seeds of capitalism's destruction. It is not only the greenhouse effect which is the product of the free play of market forces. The flood of cheap 'crack' infiltrating the Home Counties, for example, has been caused by free market entrepreneurs seeking to create and supply a demand (just as crack itself symbolises the apotheosis of unbridled capitalism – the development of a previously expensive product into a mass market affair, cheaply available to all).

The third principle is that regulation must be international. Global problems don't respect national frontiers, whether it is the spoiling of the environment, trade in illegal drugs, the spread of AIDS or the scattering of 15 million refugees in wretched camps across the world. The political problem however is that economic or political rationality never prevails per se, but only as a result of insupportable pressure. Such pressures are now foreseeable.

The exponential growth in the world's population, shown by the accelerated shortening of intervals within which the world's population has doubled, suggests that from a current level of nearly 4 billion it is unlikely to stabilise on the most optimistic control assumptions at less than three times today's level, that is 11–12 billions. It has been calculated that to raise such numbers even merely to present British or US living standards would require 12–30 times respectively the present level of industrial production. It must be extremely doubtful whether the eco-system could sustain such vastly increased demands, especially in view of the enormous rise in energy consumption required and in pollution emission per unit of production.

When over the next decades sudden resource shortages, unpredictable breakdowns or climactic destabilisation, localised at first, indicate that the eco-system cannot cope with the accelerating strains of unbridled market expansion, the growth maximisation target of the richer countries will have to be cut back. Immediately much tougher and more radical conservation and recycling techniques will be compulsorily imposed. These will represent the first serious moves towards a 'steady-state economy', where the total population and total stock of physical wealth are maintained roughly constant by physical production and consumption rates that are equal at about the lowest feasible level.

This stage would mark the beginning of the end of the so-called 'affluent society' characterised by Galbraith in its 1950s to 1970s heyday as dependent on artificial demand creation. It is here too that socialist and ecological perspectives begin to dovetail.

Industrial production would have to be geared to prior social uses, and employment and investment would need to be channelled towards the nation's most essential requirements. International planning both of the distribution of limited resource inputs and energy use, and pollution control, would become essential.

The fourth principle is that where overall expansion becomes circumscribed by ecological constraints, further development opportunities must be allotted disproportionately to poorer countries – the opposite of the 'kicking away the ladder' syndrome. Already some redistribution to the developing nations might become implicit in the latter stage just described, though it might well be made conditional on much tougher standards of population control. However, redistribution would probably be limited because no doubt pooling arrangements would be confined only to those countries directly or imminently affected.

A world can be foreseen, nevertheless, probably within a century, when the finite limit of particular resources or the finite capacity to extend industrialised processes has become demonstrably and painfully apparent. Only in such a world will national rivalries finally be absorbed into any executive international agency equipped with full powers. The ultimate implication of such an evolution is the superseding of capitalism, as a system of permanent limitless expansionism in a finite environment, and its replacement by a world-wide system of ecologically enforced priorities and choices. That is one reason why the current market domination of the economy, which perhaps reached its zenith in the 1980s, is ineluctably set to change.

4

Education and Training: the Highway to Opportunity

If people are to gain real control over their own lives and real power to influence their environment, then a radical transformation of British education and training systems – in coverage, quality and form – is perhaps the single biggest prerequisite. That means a major break from the past and the present.

Cockpit of Conflicting Ideologies

Education as a social process and function can only be defined in terms of the kind of society it is designed to serve. Over the last three decades strategies have been foisted on the education system from both left and right in pursuance of their own ulterior versions of society. Not only has neither succeeded; more importantly, neither deserves to succeed. This book proposes a new vision of society with enormous challenges for the personal development of each individual, and that will require new objectives with huge implications for the education system.

Education as Social Engineering

The achievement of a more equal and more just society through strategies of educational reform has been the liberal dream throughout the Western world since the 1950s. It offered several attractions. Equality of access to education, it was assumed, would ultimately ensure equality of access even to the highest social positions and rewards. A wider spread of skills and qualifications through the population would increase the economic bargaining power of the lower paid. And the removal of class barriers to educational success would enable the nation to utilise the full natural talents of its people, which should then increase economic growth. These were the objectives behind the popular theories of the 1960s of compensatory education (giving extra school resources to deprived children to compensate for unequal background) and of education as investment in human capital. They also underlie the great educational reports of the era led by Crowther, Robbins, Newsom and Plowden.

This social engineering package failed on two main counts. First, the relationship between social background and educational attainment – the 'iron law of social class' – proved far more intractable than anyone anticipated. Spending more on education, it turned out, benefited the already privileged far more than the disadvantaged for whom it was principally intended. The expansion of higher education in the 20 years after World War II brought an extra 1.5 per cent of children from the unskilled working classes into the universities, but at the same time an extra 13 per cent of children from the upper middle class gained entry. Such extra social mobility as has occurred in Britain in the last 30 years has resulted almost entirely from changes in the occupational structure. More people from working-class backgrounds have obtained professional and white-collar jobs simply because the number of such jobs has grown considerably. Elite groups are scarcely any more socially open than they were at the start of the century.

A second failure of the social engineering project is that it has not significantly improved the market value of unskilled or unqualified labour. It turned out that the more people possessed a particular qualification, the greater the premium on a still higher qualification. What the Americans call the 'barriers of credentialism' simply rose, leaving the lowest qualified still at the bottom. That is one prime reason why the relative income position of the bottom tenth of manual workers, at 67 per cent of the average, has hardly shifted at all in 100 years, despite much longer compulsory schooling.

Even those who provided the main political pressure behind the liberal vision became disenchanted with its results. At the political level, meritocracy, so far from eliminating inequality, simply sanctioned it in a less palatable form. Educational or social failure was now not a penalty of an unjust society, but much more clearly one's own personal shortcomings. At the private level, the monied left with their liberal consciences found more than they bargained for – their children bullied for their posh accents, or picking up working-class chauvinist attitudes, or losing interest in their violin lessons.

Faced with the liberal blind-alley, two reactions developed, again both wrong-headed. One, right-wing and popularised by Professor Jencks of Harvard, was the idea that intelligence was largely genetically determined. It probably is, but it remains true that even on the most extreme estimates of the genetic contribution to IQ, inherited ability still accounts for rather less than half educational attainment. So seeking to optimise the other factors and to reduce the disincentive effects of poor backgrounds is still relevant. The other reaction, left-wing and fostered strongly in some colleges of education, was to regard control over school values and curriculum as almost conspiratorially middle class. It was protested that what the working-class child brought to school – non-standard English and a knowledge of pigeon-fancying, vegetable gardening and football – was dismissed as of no value. At the extreme level, this led to almost blanket repudiation of the entire curriculum, which would have ruled out not only those working-class children who failed the grade, but also the minority who made it.

It is not that the social engineering experiment was wrong in principle, but rather that its potential role was misunderstood. If it is construed as an attempt to achieve social change by proxy, it will not by itself succeed. Indeed the lesson of its failure over the last 30 years is surely that if we want to redistribute wealth and power in our society, we should redistribute wealth and power by direct political means (what in fact is commonly called socialism). However, that is not to say that educational reform does not have an important role to play in conjunction with other strategic policies.

Education as a Species of Training.

The dominance of the right from the late 1970s has been reflected in the shift from a liberal visionary view of education to a strictly instrumental one. So far from being about the development of the personality in its own right, education has been equated with preparation for work in a technological society. In effect it is the industrialisation of education.

Its roots lie in Callaghan's Ruskin speech in 1976 when he urged that 'the educational system was out of touch with the fundamental need for Britain to survive economically in a highly competitive world through the efficiency of its industry and commerce'. As the Thatcherite concept of the market as the ruling force in society became dominant after 1979, this utilitarian view was rapidly converted into a range of institutions, structures and programmes reaching into the heart of the school curriculum. The introduction of the Manpower Services Commission (MSC), the Technological and Vocational Initiative (TVEI), the Certificate of Pre-Vocational Education (CPVE) and the growing range of employer–school Compacts were all designed to this end. Education is reduced to a 'factor of production' process.

The effect is social engineering in reverse: instead of education moulding the wider society of which it is part, society and the economy are determining the nature of the education system. And by bracketing education to training, it invariably involves a narrowing down of any wider consciousness to a mere mastery of certain techniques or skills. Education is no longer an opening out of the mind which transcends detail and skill and whose movement cannot be predicted. Subjects are in the curriculum as pragmatic preparation for defined jobs, not as forms of intellectual, imaginative or aesthetic inquiry.

The other key aspect of the right's training approach is the restoration of selection, in a new form, as a means of guidance to differential occupational grading within the economy. The Education Reform Act 1988 properly tackles the question of standards and a modern curriculum, though the latter is very conservatively drawn and devised without consultation with the teachers on whom, finally, high education quality depends. But testing, combined with an open enrolment policy, will have the opposite effect from raising standards. Most children will either be labelled as failures from an early age or be confined to unpopular and declining 'sink' schools. Testing at eleven, plus open (that is, selective) enrolment, equals a new eleven-plus. Further, licence to 'opt out' of Local Education Authorities to become centrally grant-aided independent schools, in due course inevitably both selective and fee-paying, represents a steady dismantling of a unitary public education system where the remaining rump will lose all credibility to sustain itself as a viable alternative.

Education as Preparation for Full Citizenhood

If education is neither an ambitious project in social engineering nor an instrumental training for employment, what *is* its role? In the light of the central theme of this book that society should be characterised by the maximum degree of power-sharing so that people gain control over their own lives to the fullest feasible extent, the purpose and function of education should be to prepare people for that exacting adult citizen role in all its widespread manifestations.

Though that might seem obvious, it is in fact a cultural tradition quite alien to Britain. The idea of education as a democratic right and a civic virtue has always been rather weak. Attitudes towards education still reflect that mixture of paternalism, deference and working-class defensiveness that was a product of the nineteenth-century education provided by the ruling class for the social and political control of the masses. Popular education has been seen as being about limiting and regulating, and expectations of mass schooling have been correspondingly low. Many working-class parents remain reluctant to get involved in schools that are experienced as alien cultural territory and for similar reasons their children readily leave school at the earliest permitted age.

Britain needs a cultural revolution in popular attitudes to education. At present we have the highest rate of early school leaving, the lowest rate of achievement in nationally recognised qualifications, and the lowest rate of participation in higher education of any country in Western Europe except Spain and Portugal. In Sweden, Japan and the US over three-quarters of students stay on in school to 17 or 18, compared with only a fifth in Britain. As a result only a quarter of British children obtain five O level passes compared with three-fifths attaining equivalent levels in Germany. Worse still, the neglect is growing. In the last decade the proportion of GNP spent on education has actually dropped by a quarter, while in the five years in the mid-1980s the staying-on rate fell by 7 per cent.

More than any other country in Europe, the British education system is exceedingly lopsided. For its brightest pupils it is elitist, with British higher education often held out as an example of excellence (despite its rigid and exclusive nature, with inflexible study programmes, part-time and mature students poorly catered for and low participation rates half the level of the US, Japan and Germany). For the rest it is not a system to rear fully-fledged citizens so much as an army of social and political pygmies. Even the vocational training alternative to the sixth form delivers low skills and lacks credibility among young people. By basing its training strategy on employers, the MSC in the past, and now the Training and Enterprise Councils (TECs), have done little more than perpetuate the English historical tradition of poor technical training which has always been workshop-based, anti-theoretical, low status and marginalised from mainstream education.

This bifurcation of the British education system derives from the precedence that has always been given to providing appropriate feedstock for carefully graded slots within the economy (a goal with a long pedigree going back to Plato's *Republic*) rather than seeking to develop a nation of rounded adults trained to handle situations and respond at whatever level of decision-making required. For a narrow capitalist ethos, the stunted growth of the majority is quite sufficient, even desirable. For a nation in which power, opportunity and self-determination is spread as widely as possible, the development of the whole person – intellectual, creative, physical and spiritual – becomes not only the right of each individual but a civic duty.

The goal is education for freedom. People are not made free when education leaves them with such a poor range of skills that a fifth of the population is forced to subsist at poverty levels. They are not free when education leaves them with such rudimentary understanding of the fundamental workings of the society around them that they are helpless to influence the decisions that dominate their lives. They are not free when the educational impact is so peripheral that their class background remains the chief determinant of their life chances. They are not free when education is seen to have little or no connection with the exercise of power and control of opportunity in society. Such people may *believe* they are free, yet their horizons are so limited and their potential so stunted that often they do not even recognise their own social or political thraldom.

A Programme for Preparation for Citizenhood for Free Men and Women

An educational policy to make people genuinely free and properly equipped to take control of their own lives must achieve *three core objectives*: it must manifestly raise standards; it must not merely introduce choice for some but restructure opportunities for everyone; and it must extend and modernise the curriculum to make it much more relevant to citizenship in the fullest sense.

Raising Standards

Diagnostic testing at regular intervals, so long as it is not used as a basis for selection, provides the obvious tool for monitoring individual performance against teacher assessment and expectations. Where it becomes apparent that pupils are falling behind in basic skills needed to complete set tasks within the curriculum, remedial assistance should be offered. This would not be a marginal activity, but might take time – up to half that spent on pupil work on the core curriculum. Concentrated and individualised attention on a pupil's identified weaknesses is a key device for raising standards all round, especially for the bottom 40 per cent of the intelligence range who at present are so readily discarded as below par.

Improving teacher morale and incentives is also a vital ingredient in raising pupil achievement. Regular checks on teaching performance and quality (including that of teacher training colleges) would provide a necessary register of professional standards, but the quid pro quo is not only better pay and conditions but more importantly improved status and greater job satisfaction. Persistent downgrading of the teachers' role by the Thatcher government, removal of negotiating rights from teachers and overloading of teachers with excessive paperwork as a result of the Baker Act have produced plummeting morale and a huge exit from the schools (20,000 teachers left the profession in 1989 alone). If their role is to be made more demanding, and it should be, then increased recognition, respect and reward is essential.

Another vital step to improving pupil standards involves harnessing a much closer link between home and school. Instead of regarding education as an oasis of compensatory schooling within a surrounding desert, community links need to be systematically developed both by visits to parents and by selected invitations of parents to the school (not merely at the annual or termly open evenings). Where a child is under-performing, such contacts should be used to analyse the reasons and to discuss the contribution the parents might make to remedy it. Such a policy will clearly require the expenditure of a great deal of teachers' time in patiently seeking to elicit parental support in the face often of indifference or even hostility, but that may be the only route to turning round a pupil's poor performance in many cases. It may well require too a significantly lower teacher–pupil ratio.

Opportunities for All, Not Just Choice for Some.

Instead of encouraging opt-outs from LEAs, draining off some select schools while leaving others to sink, reform should be aimed at upgrading not only standards but choice within the public system itself. An all-out commitment towards encouraging majority involvement in a much-widened range of education until 18 or 19 must be a priority. Perhaps the most attractive model is the Swedish gymnasiaskola which combines both academic and technical subjects for 16–19 year olds, providing multi-track routes into higher education and further training, and offering allowances to students.

Such a reform would mean abolishing the division between manual skill and brain work which both impoverishes liberal education and denigrates technique. It would also create an institutional break at 15 or 16, which would allow smaller local schools and replace the present chaos of post-16 provision with a much more rational and integrated structure (much more thorough-going than existing plans for tertiary colleges). Above all, it would give vastly greater access to higher education for traditionally excluded groups, particularly mature students, with part-time and modular courses transferable between institutions. Clearly it would require considerable extra finance and new ways of raising it should be explored, not excluding student loans partly repayable by employed graduates through income-related tax increments.

The examination framework needs radical change too. Already the National Council of Vocational Qualifications is consolidating the current array of disparate awards, but any new system would need to be integrated with the academic qualification system. There are strong arguments for abolishing the existing A levels which are far too narrow, and unnecessary as a qualification for entry into an expanded higher education system. A new form of 17+ certification needs to be developed which combines both academic and technical subjects and which is within the reach of most of the expanded numbers staying on at that level. Some form of continual assessment or credit accumulation, with or without exams, would greatly increase flexibility, choice and access.

But widening opportunities for all within the public sector cannot dodge the structural problem presented by the private schools. The continuation of a uniquely influential private sector has been deeply damaging to the state system, not only in syphoning off talent from the public sector, but also in diverting a powerful constituency from any direct interest in maintaining standards in state schools. For all their elitism, the public secondary schools of Germany and France, no less than the comprehensives of Sweden and Japan, ensure a commitment to the quality of state schooling by the main leading sections of society. A new phased programme therefore needs to be devised for integrating the private schools within the public sector, though with guarantees to preserve their quality, diversity and range.

Modernising the Curriculum

A preparation for full citizenhood for all our people, not just the chosen few, cannot duck the issue of the lack of relevance of much of the traditional school curriculum. Progressive education has been important in challenging traditional school knowledge and its class, gender and race biases, and also in developing inter-disciplinary studies and more active and critical styles of learning. But it has often failed to go beyond an ill-defined cultural relativism which assigns equal validity to all forms of knowledge and has consequently omitted to provide clear alternatives to traditional school knowledge. Further, by sometimes naively pretending that the academic curriculum can simply be bypassed and replaced by a curriculum out of knowledge that (working-class) children bring to school, the danger of the 'instant relevance' theory in 'meeting the kids where they are at' is that it forgets to take them somewhere else and leaves them excluded from the culture of power.

Two basic kinds of change urgently need to be made to the school curriculum. One is the addition of three core areas of study which are at present either totally omitted or else given only peripheral attention. These are the workings of contemporary society in Britain in terms of the economy, social mores and civic procedures, and the power structure (though obviously not parti-pris); child and human development, including psychological and emotional development, and the study of the family and domestic economy; and a basic coverage of mechanics, engineering and technology appropriate to the electronic society. The other main change required is the modernisation of the approach to traditional subjects. Perhaps the most striking example here is the treatment of history where at present far too much emphasis and time is spent on studying origins from Roman to medieval times and far too little attention is given to post-1760 Industrial Revolution economic change and to post-1945 political developments within a European and world context.

Fundamental changes in the school curriculum along these lines, delivered to all children at appropriate stages in their development and not just to a small elite, would by the age of 18 dramatically extend their perceptions of the nature of their society and of their potential role in it. Their capacity to participate in, and make a valuable contribution to, a wide spectrum of activities in the wider society, from which they are at present effectively excluded, would be enormously enhanced. The concept of democracy – rule by the people, of the people, for the people – would become a reality as never before.

In particular, the emphasis should be on the principle of community studies rather than on the teaching of discrete blocks with the traditional subject labels. This would involve pupils sometimes moving out into the community as well as outsiders with relevant expertise sometimes being brought into the school. It also means encouraging a much more imaginative and critical approach to understanding the world around rather than current over-emphasis on regurgitation of rote learning. And it means too a shift away from the present excessive concentration on academic or intellectual pursuits to a much more balanced development of the whole person including the expressive arts, crafts, sport and spiritual development.

The last, which might seem controversial, is one of the most important reforms needed. At present, the one compulsory period a week of RE (religious education) is often little more than a sad farce, leading to demands in some quarters that it be abolished altogether. The opposite is required. One of the fundamental problems of the age, particularly notable since the marked decline in religious observance in Britain around 1961, has been the loss of values and ultimate beliefs anchoring society and the individuals within it to any sense of final purpose or destiny. Materialism has run riot, at the expense of creativity, aesthetics and spirituality. Questions about the ulterior meaning and design of life – what it is all *for* – are simply brushed aside, even though in the end they cannot be evaded. In preparing people for citizenhood in a value-arid age, education has a crucial role to play in opening up these questions for scrutiny and discussion. An important part of the curriculum, and not just the one token statutory lesson, should be devoted at the appropriate ages, not merely to the study of the Christian denominations, nor even just to the world's other main religions, but to the role of religion in society, the nature of morality and ethics, and the meaning of values.

For those for whom the success of Western capitalism and the apotheosis of materialism is not, as for Francis Fukuyama, the *End of History*, the next quantum leap towards a more deeply democratic state and more enriching self-fulfilment will be in the direction of a power-sharing society. If that is so, the education system will have to be transformed out of all recognition. The programme outlined above is a minimum one for the purpose. It now needs to be explored how that more comprehensive provision of this widened range of relevant skills and knowledge will be used to bring about a new kind of state that takes forward the momentum of Western development over the last 300 years.

5

Pay

A market economy that decentralises decision-making to the individual consumer and operates via competitive markets in the production of goods and services requires, to be efficient, a distribution of effective demand among those individuals that is far different from that prevailing today. How should that be brought about?

The Nonsense of the Market as Sole Arbiter of Pay

At present, an almost mystical reverence prevails regarding pay levels set within a market economy. If that is what the market pays, so the argument runs, it must be justified. In fact, it clearly is not because in many cases market power is grossly exploited and in many other cases the market as a mechanism of supply and demand is seriously defective. Yet setting relative pay levels is absolutely fundamental in a market economy because alternative means of allocating purchasing power – like tax redistribution, social security benefits, subsidies, and vouchers – only marginally compensate for much greater inequalities already underlying. If the wealth–poverty gap is not to polarise out of control, there is no alternative to tackling market determination of pay head-on.

Market power gone riot is clearly evident when the market allots £2,512,595 in 1988 (£48,319 a week) to Mr Christopher Heath, Barings' chief bond salesman in Japan, as though he were worth *a thousand times* more than a health service worker who cleans hospital theatres for £50 a week, on the thoroughness of whose work lives may depend. Less extreme, but now far from untypical, are board chairmen like Lord Hanson and Tiny Rowland, on more than £1 million a year (nearly £20,000 a week) who are thus supposed to be worth 150 times more than the highest-paid worker in the bottom third of the workforce. It simply is not credible that they are worth *that much* more – or anything near it – than each of the 10.8 million workers now paid below the Council of Europe 'decency threshold' calculated in 1989 at £163 a week. Or if they are, then the social values underpinning such a market system must be called drastically into question.

Perks, expense accounts, restrictive practices, and tax fiddles make nonsense of any claim that market awards reflect just desserts. Huge inequalities have a lot more to do with the greed of the powerful than with incentives for the masses. In fact the market has over the years been comprehensively rigged by those who are powerful or organised against those who are neither. Market position predetermines the broad result, even before the bargaining starts, as between the different classes.

For at present four quite distinct mechanisms are used to decide pay: collective bargaining for manual workers, more personalised private negotiation for many white-collar workers, and individualised tailor-made personal contracts for senior executives, up to self-payment at the top. Equally the perspectives about these four segments of the market provide a wonderful rationale for large and growing inequality. Manual workers' pay is regarded as a cost of production, so it should be minimised to promote competitiveness. Senior executives' pay on the other hand is seen as requiring ample incentive in order to maximise their effort.

That partly explains another curiosity too. Those who start with the biggest pay also get the biggest rises. During 1979–86, average male earnings rose 16 per cent in real terms. But the increase for manual workers was only 6 per cent (including only 3 per cent for assembling, construction and mining workers). For white-collar workers however it was 22 per cent, and for professionals in management and administration it was 29 per cent. Even these figures however are dwarfed by the increases which top industrial and financial moguls award to themselves. In 1988 Tiny Rowland kept the wolf from the door by a 54 per cent pay increase which took his pay to £1,015,000 a year – a rise of £6,844 a week. Cyril Stein of Ladbrokes gave himself a pay hike of no less than 114 per cent, worth an extra £5,418 a week, and

Lord King, one of Thatcher's favourite business leaders, put up his own pay by 116 per cent. All that is to be compared with the 6 per cent awarded to bus drivers on £95 a week – a rise of only £6 a week, just *one-thousandth* as much!

How Much Inequality in Pay is Justified?

As a result of all these factors, pay differentials in 1989 were enormous.

Table 5.1: Pay differentials for 1989

Top incomes	*Pay per week (mid 1989)*
Highest paid chairmen of major companies	£19,230 plus
Highest paid barristers	£5,000 plus
Highest paid directors of large companies	£1,900 plus
Field marshal, 5 star	£1,720
Lord chief justice	£1,720
Head of the civil service	£1,720
Consultant with highest distinction awards	£1,513
General, 4 star	£1,385
High court judge	£1,385
Permanent secretary	£1,385
The high paid	
Hospital consultant, standard maximum	£757
Finance, insurance, tax specialists	£537
Medical practitioners	£512
MPs	£464
Journalists	£395
Accountants	£324
The medium paid	
Police (below sergeant)	£289
Teachers	£285
Nurse administrators	£272
Printing machine minders	£268
Firemen	£238
Car workers	£228
Machine tool operators	£206
Bus and coach drivers	£191
Registered nurses and midwives	£191
Railmen	£190
Postmen	£190

The low paid	*Pay per week (mid 1989)*
Refuse collectors	£170
Road sweepers	£162
Sales staff and shop assistants	£149
Farm workers	£146
Barmaids	£140
Typists	£139
Nursing auxiliaries	£125
Hospital ward orderlies	£122
Retail check-out operators	£109

These latest earnings figures reveal a pre-tax ratio of about 20:1 between top and bottom, from company directors to waitresses. More generally, the average professional seems to get three times, and the average director of a large company four times, the pre-tax pay of the average manual worker which in 1990 was about £235 a week.

One explanation sometimes put forward to justify these huge differences in pay is that they reflect comparative usefulness or desserts. But the facts suggest the opposite. Farm-workers, for example, on whom this country depends for much of the 55 per cent of food produced at home, earn about £146 a week on average. The average barrister, on the other hand, whose services to the community are eminently dispensable in the event of any belt-tightening, earns some £800 a week. The inference is that a lawyer is worth five or more farm labourers which is an absurdity in a world supposedly trying to gear itself to increased production rather than paper-work.

Another rationale often claimed is that pay inequalities reflect the scarcity value of particular skills: people are paid more in proportion as there are fewer persons with the required abilities. Yet that does not fit the facts either. The spread of pay from top to bottom far exceeds the range of differences that can credibly be ascribed to variations in inborn aptitudes. It is also far greater than can be accounted for by the cost of acquiring the necessary training.

Nor is it the case that jobs involving more unpleasant conditions (for example anti-social hours, dirty environment or risk of physical injury) are compensated by higher pay. In fact, the more agreeable and responsible posts win on every count. Not only is their milieu often plusher and the accompanying status and perks much more rewarding, but they are much higher paid too. Conversely, some of the most dangerous, drab and unhealthy jobs are also among the lowest paid.

Contrary to classical economic theory that variations in pay are determined primarily by market supply and demand for talent, the single most important thing that decides what people should be paid would seem to be the authority factor: those who give orders are normally better paid than those to whom such orders are given. Or to put it another way, those in positions of power ensure that pay is determined by criteria that overwhelmingly favour themselves.

The Vexed Question of Incentives

The authority principle as the determinant of pay rests on two rather curious premises. One is the sticks and carrots theory of pay. Those in authority need incentives if they are to work hard, so they always have a convenient excuse to raise their own pay. Those in subordinate positions on the other hand that lack inherent job satisfaction will not co-operate unless they are made to, so they need to be kept under constant pressure to keep their wages low. In other words, the richer you are, the more you need bigger incentives to get you to work hard, yet the poorer you are, the more you need to be deprived to get you to work hard. These contradictory principles are a major cause of the huge, and unnecessary, inequality in the spread of pay from top to bottom.

The second premise is that the exercise of authority is so burdensome that it needs to be richly compensated by high pay. In effect, people have to be bribed to take positions of power and responsibility. The empirical evidence, however, such as it is, suggests the opposite. Surveys have regularly shown that when asked to rank in order what they seek from work, people do not rate pay first. They regularly place it behind their aspirations for job satisfaction, the exercise of power or responsibility, and social status.

Moreover, the disincentive effect of progressive taxation on high earners has been greatly exaggerated. For high tax rates have been offset by a string of extremely generous tax allowances and reliefs. That is why, though the top income tax rate of 83 per cent in 1979 was vitriolically complained of, only 1 in every 500 taxpayers actually paid it. It is also why even the highest paid still retained 70 per cent of their gross salary even after paying these 'crippling' rates of tax. More importantly, recent research for the treasury by Professor CV Brown of Edinburgh University has shown that higher taxes, so far from providing a disincentive to work, can more likely give an incentive to *greater* work. People will try to recoup their losses from higher taxes by increasing their earnings, that is by working longer hours or taking on extra work.

Huge inequalities are by no means necessary therefore to create incentives – indeed they may be counter-productive and generate the opposite effect. Thus it can scarcely be justified that in 1990, when workers on average earnings got an increase of 9.5 per cent which worked out at £27 a week, 4 million low-paid workers earning less than half male median earnings received an average rise of 6 per cent or about £7 a week, while at the other end of the scale the highest-paid executives in a survey of a quarter of Britain's top 100 companies got average salary increases of 33 per cent which amounted (given that their average pay already stood at £380,000 a year) to an extra £2,411 a week. So top executives in 1990 received gross pay increases 344 times greater than the lowest-paid seventh of the workforce. All this has a lot more to do with the greed of the powerful than with incentives for the masses.

Moreover, tax policy, so far from mitigating these effects, has actually exaggerated them. The cumulative effect of the budget strategy 1979–90 on the distribution of incomes was shown in a Parliamentary Answer on 3 April 1990. The government revealed that the poorest on incomes of under £100 a week were £2 a week better off as a result of changes in tax reliefs, while the top-paid 1 per cent with incomes over £70,000 a year were now £693 a week better off as a result of tax gains since 1979. Ironically the differential gain between top and bottom was again about the same – 346 to 1.

Indeed there is a real perversity in the current spread of incentives. Those who need them most – at the bottom of the pile – have them least. Thus while the top marginal rate for high earners was halved in the Thatcher decade from 83 per cent to 40 per cent, there was a steady increase to over 350,000 in the number of very low earners who according to government figures have to pay a poverty trap marginal rate of over 80 per cent. At the other end there has been an even sharper growth in the concentration of perks and wealth at the top. According to Inland Revenue figures, the average person in the richest 1 per cent of the population is now 175 times richer than the average person in the poorer half of the nation. If anyone needs real incentives, it is surely those at the bottom.

Distributing Pay Fairly

For all these reasons it is one of the great deceits of our time that a market basis for determining pay must be fair and right. In fact, the comprehensive control over pay systems exerted by business and professional elites, particularly at the top and bottom ends, ensures that pay determination is at present as much a matter of power as of economic efficiency or social fairness. So what should be done to bring a much stronger element of real efficiency and justice into the whole issue of deciding pay and providing incentives? It is a question that translates into how can matters of pay be opened up to much wider influences throughout the population?

Establishing Fair Differentials

First a new institution is needed for the systematic launch and development of a major public debate about pay. What rung on the ladder of incomes do people in different occupations think they should occupy compared with people in other walks of life, and what do other people feel *their* job should be worth? Ironically, the Tories themselves started this process in 1973 when they set up their Relativities Commission to find a way out of their dispute with the miners. The Commission was told to examine how much miners were worth in relation to postmen, dustmen and so on. Its brief did not embrace such dangerous ideas as the relative value of miners compared with High Court judges, Fleet Street journalists, advertising executives or university professors. But that is exactly what does need to be openly discussed.

A new commission, or whoever leads the public debate, should propose alternative systems of rewards which reflect justice and efficiency rather than market criteria based on decades of organised strength or centuries of accumulated privilege. The new criteria would take into account such principles as: skills involved in the work, the length of training, conditions in the workplace, unsocial hours (for example shift work, night work, holiday working), physical or mental exertion, degree of responsibility and how socially useful is the work.

The Pay Relativities Commission should not be merely an external arm of government solely used in a crisis for the resolution of disputes. It should have a relatively open-ended brief to examine pay comparisons, not merely at the behest of ministers, but at the request of other representative organisations. For opening up the triggering of such investigations to general public demand should over time mould the country's pay structure much more closely to the rationale of public opinion and agreed social values.

Whole Company Pay Bargaining

The Thatcher government demanded flexibility in pay bargaining, but interpreted that far too narrowly. It was meant to signify a shift from over-rigid national pay determination to more varied local pay systems. But that meets only one aspect of Britain's inflexible pay structure – broadly how the pay of manual workers should be fixed. It omits other dimensions like the maintenance of large historical differentials between non-manual and manual grades and the different procedures for pay determination according to status level. Flexibility therefore needs to be taken a great deal further.

This should be done by basing pay awards across the board on new principles that genuinely reflect job evaluation and performance rating by those with direct knowledge and experience, namely those working at other levels in the same organisation. Representatives of all the main grades within the enterprise (or each major self-sufficient unit) should meet at least once a year; in small organisations, with 20 or less employees, it might be expected they would all meet together as a whole. They would open the books, review the financial position of the enterprise (debt, depreciation, stock provision, dividends, investment, cash flow, etc.), and then determine the funding availability for pay increases throughout the organisation. Each representative of each group would make the case for a certain pay increase for their own group. What was finally awarded to each group would depend on the decision of all the other representatives jointly, on the basis of course that the more that was allotted to one group, the less would be available for others.

Such a framework for deciding pay increases has enormous merits. Instead of the selfish pursuit of sectional interests by each group regardless of the welfare of the organisation overall, it would require each group to relate its own interests to those of others and to the enterprise as a whole. Instead of pay deals being cooked up in smoke-filled rooms or in private negotiations behind closed doors, the whole process would be transparent. Instead of pay being seen as spoils to be maximised in a constant market struggle, it would for the first time be seen as an expression of relative worth, to be explained and argued for publicly. Above all, instead of pay being an instrument of power exerted by leaders over all the subordinate groups within their organisations, it becomes a joint decision for those groups themselves, a decentralisation of power among those directly affected, though firmly subject to all the necessary economic realities.

There are several obvious objections. One is that it would remove the traditional role of the trade unions as the agents of collective bargaining. In fact the unions' role radically changes, but remains equally important. They would be responsible for research and back-up to strengthen their representatives' case, and while industrial action would become a last rather than a first resort, withdrawal of labour would always remain the final option in a free society, and it would require union support to organise it. Another objection is that it would encounter strong management resistance. In fact it would force managers to rely less on pay-fixing structural authority and more on a skills-based appeal, and all the more healthy for that. Senior management would undoubtedly still get bigger pay rises than the average, but they would have to argue for it openly on grounds of scarce top-level skills, not simply pay themselves fancy salaries in private.

This proposal meets the criteria both of the market *and* of fairness. If the enterprise was to succeed, those with needed scarce skills would still have to be bid for at a premium within an open market system. But the pressure from below to maximise incentives *throughout* the organisation and not only in the higher reaches would mean that any such special pleading would be restrained to the minimum strictly necessary. To that extent this proposed framework would over time be a force for reducing the excesses towards indefensible degrees of inequality at both ends of the income spectrum. It would operate to maintain inequalities, but no more than those that could be rationally justified.

Minimum and Maximum

Whole-company pay bargaining would constrain and gradually reduce the extremities in the range of incomes where these were not warranted. However, it is doubtful if it would work far enough within a short enough time to eliminate the indefensible excesses at both top and bottom of the range. While pay over much of the middle strata is quite finely calibrated to match market signals reflecting differential skills, there is clearly no such rationale at the extremes. It is not obvious why many nurses, farm workers and garbage collectors, all of whom perform essential roles, are paid less than half, sometimes only a third, of the national average wage, while advertising executives, tax accountants and army generals may be paid 5 times the national average, and some chief executives are awarded a quixotic 70 times the national average.

There is therefore a very strong case for squeezing the income distribution at both ends. At the bottom, since neither collective bargaining nor Wages Councils nor greater tax progressivity have been shown to improve the lot of the very low-paid more than marginally, the case for minimum wage legislation seems unanswerable. Britain is in fact alone in the EEC in offering no legal protection for the lowest paid: all the other countries provide either a statutory minimum floor or a legal extension of collective agreements to unorganised workplaces.

A minimum wage in the UK fixed at half male median earnings would establish a minimum rate of pay, pro rata for part-time workers, of £3.40 per hour or £129 a week. It would increase the pay of about 4 million workers. Three objections in the main have been raised against this: that it would be inflationary, cause unemployment and undermine efficiency. The cost effects have been variously estimated at 3–5 per cent of the national wage bill, and foreign studies (for example in Canada) suggest indirect costs in addition amounting to some 60 per cent of direct costs. That would indicate a total cost, including the repercussive knock-on on differentials, of some 5–8 per cent of the wage bill. But even if it were as much as 10 per cent, then on the basis that wages represent about two-thirds of total industrial costs, prices would rise about 6–7 per cent. If then this process were phased in over three years, the inflationary impact would be about 2 per cent a year for three years. That is surely a tolerable price to pay to ensure that several million low-paid workers and their families achieved at least the minimum purchasing power so that the market economy operates with reasonable fairness.

Nor in most cases does low pay exist because employers cannot afford to pay more. Together with retailing, catering accounts for the largest concentration of low-paid jobs in the economy. Yet during the 1984–9 boom the hotels and catering industry doubled its profits to more than £2.25 billion a year. Both retailing and catering are now dominated by large, often multi-national, conglomerates that are highly profitable. This applies too in sectors like contract cleaning where low pay is very widespread.

Claims that a statutory minimum wage increases unemployment are not borne out by international experience. France, the Netherlands and Belgium, whose minimum wage is around 60 per cent of male median earnings (significantly higher than the 50 per cent proposed for Britain), do not report higher unemployment on this count. Indeed a minimum wage can actually *increase* overall employment because it raises the level of total demand which should generate jobs elsewhere within the economy.

Again, arguments that a minimum wage saps efficiency are the reverse of the truth.

It was formerly supposed that the workings of supply and demand would naturally regulate or eliminate that evil (of payment below a living wage). But where you have no organisation, no parity of bargaining, the good employer is undercut by the bad and the bad employer is undercut by the worse.

No trade union leader, but Mrs Thatcher's exemplar, Winston Churchill, in a speech to the Commons on 28 April 1909. Indeed, industries which come to rely on cheap labour provide a way by which inefficient producers and obsolete technologies can compete: they can force down wages and conditions of work in order to survive. Competition should be based on quality of product, design or productive efficiency. Low pay imposes economic costs in terms of technological backwardness, reduced productivity, and lower standards of service to the consumer.

Moreover, the EEC proposal in 1991 to introduce a Minimum Wage Directive removed any idea that Britain would be internationally disadvantaged. Once again, the truth is the opposite. *Other* EEC countries are not prepared to tolerate *Britain* using low wages as a form of hidden subsidy or tariff to give UK firms an unfair competitive edge. The Germans in particular strongly oppose 'social dumping'. If low wages are necessary to the British economy, it does not show how well the market is working, it shows how *badly* it is working.

What of the other end of the spectrum? According to a labour research survey, the number of company directors paid more than £100,000 a year rose to 2,500 in 1989, while 78 topped the £0.5 million mark and 14 exceeded even the £1 million mark. Is there a case for a maximum pay limit, say five times the national average wage (which would yield £77,000 in 1990)? The rationale would be three-fold. Annual pay exceeding a quarter of a million, or even £100,000, grossly outstrips any objective criterion of relative social worth. Its extravagance undermines any public sense of fairness in overall pay scales. And calls for restraint, when economic times get tough, are difficult to sustain when a hyper-rich minority are so patently insulated from sacrifices demanded of others. Something therefore has to be done. However, a fixed and arbitrary limit for top pay would inevitably be over-rigid. So a short sharp attack to reduce the grotesque and indefensible extremes at the top might best be delivered via an excess charge levied at perhaps 75 per cent on incomes above some multiple (say five, which would embrace roughly the 1 per cent highest paid of earners) of national average earnings.

Sharing out the 'Fringe Benefits' Goldmine

If people are to gain real control over their own lives and therefore need the purchasing power to express their will effectively without an intolerable excess of inequality in the market-place, that must apply to all remuneration, not just some. It must certainly apply to what are euphemistically called 'fringe benefits'. They are not fringe, but major portions of total remuneration, and they are not benefits for all, but thinly disguised tax evasion for the few.

The latest survey of executive 'perks' (by P-E International, 1990) reveals that among managing directors (average total money pay of £103,000), 97 per cent received from their company full use of a company car, 42 per cent had subsidised lunches, 57 per cent had a subsidised private phone, 12 per cent had help with housing, 97 per cent had life assurance, 92 per cent had free medical insurance, 36 per cent enjoyed executive share options, 22 per cent benefited from profit-sharing schemes, 8 per cent received loans at low interest, and 55 per cent were paid a bonus (which amounted to 21 per cent of the average salary of those receiving it). For managerial executives at all levels, the percentages in each case were naturally lower, but only slightly so. Amongst the managed, however, these perks are very limited or non-existent.

Two reforms are needed. One is that fringe benefits should be recognised for what they are – devices to reward high-paid employees outside the tax system – and their worth then evaluated in monetary terms and taxed at the beneficiary's marginal rate. The other is that the secret world of perks should be opened up and made the subject of whole company pay bargaining as much as the pay negotiations themselves. That would block the monopoly on lucrative perks at the top, and ensure they were distributed throughout the organisation in amounts that could be justified as incentives for all.

In summary, the combination of all these measures would radically transform the spread of purchasing power throughout society. Instead of the market, whatever efficiency it might entail, being a constant source of injustice because of the excessive and indefensible inequalities it generated, this new framework would bring social pressures systematically to bear on pay determination. It would thus steadily produce a narrower and much more justifiable spread of incomes, without loss of market flexibility. Since money is so much the source of power, this would go a long way to disseminating power and opportunity much more evenly between individuals.

6

Control Over the Politicians

We are very proud of our Western democracy. But how democratic really is it? In constitutional theory it hinges on the right of the electorate to choose a government every four to five years, which is then assisted by an impartial civil service and proceeds to implement the manifesto on which it was elected. On every count however this liberal democratic facade is seriously flawed. In particular, the decentralisation of power, or the degree of accountability, to ordinary citizens is minimal. It is today almost as significant a question as it was 300 years ago: how does the populace exercise power over the normal power-holders of society? Any real intention therefore that people should command genuine control of their own political destiny will require a series of far-reaching reforms in the power structure of Britain.

Ending Elective Dictatorship

'The power of the Prime Minister has grown, is still growing, and should be cut back,' wrote Richard Crossman in his *Diaries* in the 1960s. Since his warning then the process has gone a great deal further. In 1977 Lord Hailsham described a system where government 'took advantage of the virtually absolute sovereignty of the House of Commons to behave in a manner that is undeniably anti-democratic'. He called such a system an 'elective dictatorship', and was referring to the Labour government of the 1970s, but there could scarcely be a more apt description of the Thatcher years. Mrs Thatcher's imperious dominance of political power throughout her long reign 1979–90 destroyed the constitutional nicety of cabinet government whereby the prime minister was merely 'primus inter pares' and raised the spectre of autocracy despite all the traditional democratic trappings.

Only in Britain is there such a concentration of power at a single centre without effective counter-checks. In America there is a carefully contrived division of power between president and congress, with the president often having to negotiate with an opposing political party in control of Capitol Hill. In France the president is elected separately from the assembly and may have to 'cohabit' with a prime minister politically opposed to him (for example during 1983–5). In Germany, power is balanced between the centre and the partly autonomous state governments.

Only in Britain are the roles of executive head of state and prime minister combined, while at the same time almost untrammelled political power is concentrated in a single parliamentary assembly dominated by the prime minister's party machine. Such a system may work in Britain when political leaders do not press their powers to excess and welcome, or at least tolerate, diversity; it breaks down when potential checks and balances are eliminated. The Thatcher experience forces on to the agenda a fundamental re-assessment of the whole balance of power within a so-called democracy.

It showed that the greatest threat to freedom in Britain in the 1980s and 1990s is posed by the development of an over-mighty executive. It dominates the House of Commons, which now exercises too little restraint on ministers. So long as it enjoys a comfortable majority, it can pass a great deal of legislation of which the House does not really approve, can almost always destroy any independent back-bench initiative, and can take many vitally important actions without even telling the House at all. It can outface the House of Lords which may be an irritant, but is no real check. With a prime minister who is prepared to be ruthless, as Thatcher was, it can subordinate or at least neutralise all other independent centres of power like the judiciary, the press, the universities, local government, the trade unions and the churches.

Sitting at the apex of this structure of unaccountable power is the prime minister. He or she can appoint and dismiss ministers, with no constitutional requirement to have these confirmed by parliament; can create peers and dispense honours; and controls leading appointments in the civil service, diplomatic service, armed forces, security services, public sector industry and the church. The prime minister also has complete personal control of the conduct of government business: which items are to be discussed in cabinet and which excluded, the power to set up cabinet committees and appoint their members, and the power to circulate or withhold cabinet committee papers from other cabinet members. The prime minister also by dint of personal responsibility for the security services can have any person, including ministers, put under surveillance. And by use of the prerogative powers of the crown the prime minister can dissolve parliament before the end of its natural term, thus pre-empting the most suitable moment for an election.

A linked series of reforms is therefore needed before the excessive and over-dominant power of the premiership in Britain, and the over-mighty executive he or she leads, is reduced by the necessary democratic balances. They include tackling the pervasive and corrupting system of patronage wielded by the prime minister, the undue power of the whips or party managers, the unreasonable degree of secrecy of the government machine, reform of the Lords to make the second chamber a real balance, and the rights of the electorate via referenda, as well as the whole vexed question of electoral reform. Each of these is now examined, not only as reforms in their own right, but as contributions to the overall reformulation of political power in Britain and to the real objective of transferring power to the people.

Restricting Patronage – the Opium of the Elite

The prime minister has at his or her command more patronage than a medieval monarch. First, he or she appoints all ministers, both in the cabinet and outside. Over a recent 30 year period seven prime ministers made 1,494 ministerial appointments, including 309 to the cabinet. The prime minister can also dismiss ministers, and the regime of fear engendered by a ruthless use of this power can muffle dissent or even debate. By 1990 all the 21 members of Thatcher's original 1979 cabinet had either resigned or been sacked. The prime minister creates peers: over the last 30 years 568 hereditary or life peers were created. In addition there are all the other honours. In the 64 New Year and monarch's Birthday lists over these 30 years, the seven prime ministers created 118 baronetcies and 264 knighthoods.

The prime minister is also consulted personally on appointments of all chairmen of nationalised industries, and there were 85 such key appointments in those 30 years. The prime minister is also consulted on the appointment of all permanent secretaries, the leading players in the government machine – posts which Thatcher notoriously tried to restrict to those of her own ideology, 'one of us' – as well as on almost all top appointments to positions of influence throughout public life. If one assumes that there are two or three hopefuls for every successful candidate for an honour or a top appointment, seven post-war prime ministers extended their influence over between 5,000 and 7,000 would-be ministers, lords, knights and chairmen – quite apart from the prime minister's role in choosing archbishops, bishops and judges.

The honours system is invidious, divisive and deeply corrupting. At root it is an insidious means of buying loyalty and manipulating the surrounding elites. Patronage secures obedience, and what patronage cannot secure directly, honours buy indirectly. The most important power centre outside the public service with the key role of influencing public opinion is the media, particularly newspapers. Significantly, editors favouring her cause were lavishly rewarded by Thatcher. Sir Larry Lamb of the *Sun*, Sir John Junor of the *Mail on Sunday*, Sir David English of the *Daily Mail*, Lord Matthews of Express Newspapers, Lord Stevens of United Newspapers, and in her resignation list Sir Nick Lloyd of the *Daily Express* have all had their devotion recognised. It was the slavishness of much of Fleet Street, combined with the neutering of her cabinet and the majority of her back-bench MPs (she gave ten times as many knighthoods to Tory back-benchers as did Heath), which allowed Thatcher to exercise such an unhealthy degree of power.

Even more crudely, honours are used by prime ministers, since the days of Lloyd George, to raise funds. During Thatcher's premiership, 17 private sector industrialists were made peers. Between them they contributed more than £5 million to the Tory Party or its front organisations like British United Industrialists – that is, £300,000 per peerage. Research by John Walker in his book *The Queen has been pleased* found that Thatcher had created more knights than for 70 years, and that two-thirds of these new knights were employed by companies which had contributed £11 million to Tory funds, roughly £150,000 per knighthood. Moreover, those companies which had given most in funds also received most in honours. In Thatcher's first term 1979–83, the ten companies which contributed £200,000 or more to Tory Party funds received no fewer than six peerages and five knighthoods.

The whiff of corruption goes deeper. The chairman of one of Britain's largest companies, who had been publicly critical of the government's industrial policies, claimed his company had been consistently discriminated against in the award of contracts. Competitors, who had paid their political dues and kept quiet, were rewarded in a variety of ways, including honours.

For all these reasons, if power within the political process is to be more widely spread, then the excessive and unhealthy power of the prime minister must be diminished, and as a main means to that end the honours system should be abolished. Its insidious corrupting influence in so many ways overwhelmingly exceeds its positive use, and its manipulation by a ruthless prime minister is extremely damaging to a free political system.

Second, the power of patronage to exercise indirect control over surrounding elites should be curtailed. While it may appeal to insiders – as one mandarin put it, 'patronage is second only to the act of love in conferring pleasure on all parties concerned' – it can often pervert proper democratic instincts: pleasing the leader becomes more important than representing constituents or sticking to an unpopular cause. What is needed is a new framework for handling all top appointments within public life: while the prime minister or other senior ministers may propose a name, it should be for parliament in open public hearings either to ratify it or reject it. The appropriate departmental select committee should be convened for a thorough investigation of the ministerial appointee in front of the TV cameras, as in the congressional confirmation hearings in the US. The appointment is only ratified if the person commands a majority vote of confidence on the committee. Such open examinations would not only curb ministerial patronage, they would also subject key state appointments to the full force of public opinion.

Opening up Parliament to the Popular Will

The liberal constitutional concept that an electoral vote every five years secures government in accordance with the will of the people is hopelessly flawed. The truth is very different on several

counts. One is the whipping system which ensures that whatever
is decided by the cabinet, or even by a strong prime minister
dominating cabinet, will invariably carry the day in both
Commons and Lords, whatever the reservations of individual
members and whatever the opposition in the country. A three-line
(that is, compulsory) whip is not confined to policy votes of
strategic significance to the party, but permeates voting on items
of much lesser magnitude which are not covered by any electoral
mandate. Tightness of party control has far outstripped adherence to the popular will.

Another issue is that governments do not regard themselves as
bound by their manifestos. They frequently initiate major changes
of policy direction (and not only where emergencies or unfore-
seen events require it) for which they have no electoral sanction.
prime ministers, once elected, like to see themselves as mandated
to take their own decisions untrammelled.

Another divergence of reality from theory concerns the
increasing autocracy of party leaders within a supposedly
collegiate system. Thatcher illustrated this most clearly. She built
up a policy unit in No. 10 which regularly second-guessed
ministers, plus an immediate coterie of unelected advisers,
notably Powell and Ingham, who by dint of constant access to the
prime minister (indeed her unofficial gate-keepers) exercised
more power than cabinet ministers. With her connivance Ingham
even gave press briefings against elected ministers to convey
official displeasure. A similar pattern developed in the opposition, with Clarke and Mandelson performing a comparable role
for Neil Kinnock. It represents a major departure from democratic
accountability at the top of politics. In the case of both government
and opposition, initiatives in both party management and policy
direction originate in personal circles round the leader, who then
uses his or her position – invoking a mixture of patronage, loyalty
and fear – to push what had been privately agreed through the
official machine.

A fourth issue which makes parliament, not an arbiter for the
people, but merely a sounding board for the controllers of the
government machine is that many of the most important
decisions bypass parliament (and some even the cabinet)
altogether. Examples include the decision by the Attlee government about 1947 to manufacture the atomic bomb, by Heath to

establish internment without trial in Northern Ireland in 1972, by Callaghan to 'modernise' the Polaris nuclear warhead in 1977 and by Thatcher to sanction the bombing of Libya in 1985 by US warplanes based in Britain. Many of the key decisions – leaving aside genuine issues of national security – concerning foreign policy, defence and particularly nuclear policy, Northern Ireland, and City finance are never debated in Parliament, and indeed in a number of cases parliament is not even informed such decisions have been taken.

A fifth problem is that, when all else fails, government may resort to use of the 'royal prerogative'. The sovereign personally has effective power over only two prerogatives: the right to dissolve parliament and to remove a government (used against Gough Whitlam in Australia in 1975), and the right to ask somebody to form a government (vital in a hung parliament). All other crown prerogatives are effectively sub-contracted to the prime minister who can use them without consulting either cabinet or parliament. The powers of the crown exercised by the prime minister include the right to declare war, to make peace, to sign or ratify treaties, to grant pardons, to grant charters, to confer honours, to make appointments, to establish commissions, and to issue orders. The Thatcher government extended the use of the royal prerogative to avoid proper democratic control in several sensitive areas, for example the unilateral removal in 1984 of the rights of civil servants at GCHQ to belong to a trade union, the sanctioning of MI5 to enter, search, burgle and bug premises and be exempt from prosecution, and the alleged RUC shoot-to-kill policy in Northern Ireland.

Altogether these derogations from parliamentary sovereignty make the idea of Parliament as the guardian of democracy into at best a charade and at worst a complete myth. If parliament is really to perform its allotted role as the forum where all key national decisions are openly taken in an elected assembly accountable to the people, several reforms are required. None is sufficient by itself, but collectively they would go far to countervail the power of the over-mighty executive.

The departmental select committees should have the right to summon ministers and to subpoena all relevant documents (subject only to strict considerations of national security) which would open up the workings of government in a way no other

method could achieve. Their ultimate sanction should be to issue
a report of censure on a minister, which would then require a full
debate on a motion of censure on the minister on the floor of the
House. If passed, the minister would be deprived of his post.
Failure to attend the committee or to comply with its reasonable
requests, or attempting to bypass the proper procedures of
parliament, would put a minister at risk of these penalties. Such
a reassertion by the legislature of its traditional right to check the
executive would also have the salutary consequence of making a
minister answerable less to prime ministerial patronage and more
to parliament.

The prime minister should be made accountable to parliament
in three main ways. Where he or she acts directly and specifically
in any departmental area (like Thatcher's personal authorisation
of the US bombing of Libya from the UK), the prime minister
should be answerable to the relevant select committee, and liable
to the same sanctions, as the cabinet minister heading that
department. Where the prime minister (or other cabinet minister)
makes major public appointments, they should be subject to
ratification, or rejection, by the appropriate select committee. And
where the prime minister makes lesser (that is non-cabinet)
appointments, allocates portfolios or makes party management
(including his or her private office personnel) dispositions, they
should in every case be subject to consultation and agreement
with back-bench party leaders, whether those appointed by the
PLP and NEC in the case of the Labour Party or the 1922
committee in the case of the Tory Party.

These reforms would make the executive genuinely accountable to the legislature, which would itself be subject to dual
accountability both to the party via re-selection and to the
electorate at general elections. They would make the whole
government machine much more responsive to the popular will.
However, where parliament still fails for whatever reason to meet
popular aspirations over a key issue, the constitutional right to a
referendum should be made available. The idea is resisted in
Britain, but there are plenty of precedents. The Swiss hold
referenda on many issues, big and small; so do Americans, in their
individual states. Denmark had a referendum on signing up for
the Single European Act that would bring in much more majority
voting between EEC governments. Norway had a referendum on

whether to join the EEC. Britain itself had referenda on Scottish and Welsh devolution in 1977, as well as in 1975 on the negotiated terms for continued membership of the EEC (though the latter somewhat brought the idea into disrepute because it was used primarily to resolve a deep internal party split).

The case for referenda on major, especially constitutional, issues is that some matters are of such surpassing importance (for example the federalist implications of a 'single currency' in stage three the Delors plan, or the de-nuclearisation of the country's defence capability) that the authorisation of a specific national vote is required. A single vote at a general election every five years cannot possibly discriminate individual preferences over the whole range of key questions. If democracy is to be real, and not merely a constitutional facade whereby the government claims a mandate for whatsoever it does, more specific consultation of the electorate, on carefully chosen categories of policy and on proven evidence of a national demand (for example a petition with half a million signatures, 1 per cent of the electors), is essential.

Getting Control of the Whitehall Machine

If the people of Britain are to get political decision-making that really reflects their interests, then major reform of the civil service is needed too. For at present government departments are notoriously secretive, elitist and self-contained with their own traditional view of how things should be done ('the man in Whitehall knows best').

There are several ways in which leading officials, not conspiratorially but as a matter of habit and procedure, subvert the democratic vote. One is the manipulation of individual ministers, an exercise in person-management which is skilfully orchestrated and on which a great deal of time and care is spent. Another is the political isolation of ministers and the resulting dependence on the Whitehall machine, for which a heavy price in policy terms is paid. Yet another is the exploitation of the inter-departmental committee system, the real power-house inside Whitehall, which can be used to circumvent ministers who may be opposing the consensus of officialdom.

A fourth factor is the close inter-lock with establishment

interests outside, which can mean officials are acting in concert with the extra-parliamentary power structure against ministers rather than in support of the political manifesto of the governing party. A fifth is the selective restriction on the dissemination of information, which keeps the power of decision-making limited in fewer hands and rebuts undesired ministerial or public intrusion, especially into the most sensitive areas of policy. And a sixth is the poor quality of advice to Ministers, being preoccupied with advocacy rather than analysis, hostility to change, neglect of the long term, failure to perceive issues across institutional boundaries and adherence to the bureaucratic consensus whatever the political manifesto may say.

To enable the rest of society therefore to exert real influence over Whitehall deliberations, several changes need to be made. Perhaps the most important is a Freedom of Information Act which would prevent the mandarins monopolising the power of decision-making behind the curtains of secrecy. Probably 80 per cent of classified documents could, and should, be opened up to the public domain without any loss of efficiency or security to government. Never again would arrogant officials be found saying: 'If you knew what I know, you would not ask a silly question like that!' No other single act would over time so dramatically transform people from passive onlookers in a Big Brother state to informed and participatory fully fledged citizens.

If ministers as political tribunes of the people (not mere ciphers of patronage or proteges of the prime minster) are to give a strong political direction to their departments, they need more than a couple of political advisers (the limit permitted at present), personally chosen from outside Whitehall for their specialist expertise, to give effective steerage to an army of ten thousand officials in their department. They need at least half a dozen or more to act as progress chasers, meeting the minister at the start of each day to review the past day's progress and to plan the next day's drive. They should act as the minister's 'eyes and ears' within the department, and for that purpose should have routine access to the inter-departmental official committees which are the real engine house in Whitehall.

The promotion, transfer or allocation of civil servants should be taken out of the hands of a cosy inner circle of top permanent secretaries. Ministers should have the right to choose their own leading officials with whom they can work effectively and comfortably, not be forced to work with those who go out of their way to obstruct and who are ideologically incompatible (like Tony Benn with Sir Anthony Part at the Department of Industry in 1974). That would switch the basic loyalty of junior officials to ministers, whom electors have put in charge, rather than to permanent secretaries who may be pursuing a very different agenda.

Checks and Balances to Reflect the Will of the People

All these reforms together would enable the population to exert far more cogent influence on those who govern them, and would irreversibly shift the balance of power towards those who, directly or indirectly, could be held to account by the electorate. However, ending the drift of the last few decades towards elective dictatorship demands a more fundamental structural check on the ever-growing power of the prime minister. One means to achieve this which is becoming increasingly fashionable is proportional representation (PR).

It is claimed that PR is 'fairer', in that parties get a share of MPs more directly proportional to their national vote. Under first-past-the-post, Thatcher was able to lord it over the country for a decade after getting only 42–44 per cent of the vote in three successive elections, while the Liberals got 26 per cent of the national vote in 1983, but won only 2 per cent of parliamentary seats. If election to Westminster were based on PR, the Thatcherite imperium might never have happened.

In fact PR is neither more nor less democratic than the existing electoral system. It is simply different, with certain advantages, but also considerable disadvantages. Instead of a clear overall majority after an election, a government would very likely only emerge after intensive back-stairs bargaining between the parties, behind the backs of the voters. The final government programme might very well bear little resemblance to the actual policies put before the electorate by the separate parties. Then as coalitions ebb and flow, the real political debate moves from the public arena to the private so that, as happened for example in West Germany in 1982, governments can even change hands without any consultation with the voters. Moreover, the vital links between specific communities and their elected MPs would be severely weakened if the latter were chosen through Party lists or giant multi-member constituencies.

Under PR the almost certain need to construct coalitions would have the opposite defect to the present system – it would give undue power to small unrepresentative parties. Through their power to make or break coalitions, they could insist on highly sectional policies that have little real support in the country (the tiny religious parties in Israel are a case in point). Meanwhile, much larger parties may be completely excluded from power. In fact, PR is largely a mechanism for securing a permanent Centrist coalition to govern Britain. It would be almost certain to strengthen considerably the forces of the status quo, which is its main attraction for the City, Fleet Street and the Whitehall establishment.

If PR is therefore not an effective instrument for ensuring the political will of the people prevails better than now, is there another route which would better secure this objective, while at the same time reversing the drift towards elective dictatorship? This could be met by the replacement of the present House of Lords by a regionally elected second chamber.

The House of Lords is a patent anachronism. Built on the hereditary principle, unaccountable to the people, grossly imbalanced in party loyalties, it contains some 963 registered peers of whom less than half, about 392, are defined as 'working peers', that is those who turn up one day in three. While useful in scrutinising some legislation and more independent of the whips than the Commons, it can never perform the role of checking an over-dominant executive, particularly a Conservative one.

A second chamber to replace the Lords should be elected on a regional basis, not least because regional polarisation increasingly threatens the break-up of the UK. The electoral base might consist of seven regions of roughly equal population – which might be Scotland, Wales, the North, the Midlands, the South-west, the South-east and London – three of which might normally be expected to vote Labour and three Tory, with London as a swing region. There should be direct elections by the people as a whole in the region, not nominations or indirect elections by devolved regional assemblies or regional councils, needed though these are to decentralise power from London.

The elected second chamber would be able to initiate lesser legislation, to revise legislation, and to delay its enactment. But its main function would be to protect civil freedoms and ensure that no legislation promoted by the government infringed rights enshrined in prior legislation. There should be no ministers on its benches, and no need for party machines to whip their members according to tight party lines. Its members should be precluded from government office, so they should be expected to be ruggedly independent of promoting government interests. It should be elected on a first-past-the-post framework, on the principle that any governmental body that initiates legislation or has statutory executive functions should reflect such a voting system.

One final check to ensure the will of the electorate prevails lies in limiting the disproportionate power of money to subvert the democratic vote. The inequality in financial power between the two sides in the EEC referendum in 1975 was eleven to one, and in general elections it varies around five to one in favour of the Tory Party. Given that there is also extreme imbalance in the press in the same direction, there is an overwhelming case for setting a ceiling for party expenditure in general elections. At present, spending per candidate is strictly limited, which is irrelevant when campaigns are decided almost exclusively at national level. Total party expenditure should therefore be kept to a limit of, say, £5 million in order that sheer weight of funding should not score an undemocratic advantage.

In summary, if people are to acquire the power to control their own lives, the political power structure, where at present lines of accountability to the people are very tenuous, must be fundamentally re-organised. If democracy is to be for real, then one vote every five years is merely the foundation. A series of channels of influence need to be built so that a better informed and more assertive electorate, can intervene effectively as and when it wishes in the political process. The reforms outlined here are the minimum for that purpose.

7

Power Under the Law:
Equal Rights and Civil Liberties

We are all equal under the law. Or are we? Where people get involved in disputes over the rent or housing conditions, social security rights, personal or matrimonial issues, immigration access, harassment or dismissal by an employer, or any other of the regular day-to-day areas of potential conflict, do they feel able to exert pressure against those persons or bodies that encroach on their lives? If not, how can they acquire that power?

Current Restrictions on Access to Justice

In fact, at present, if individuals' power to exercise effective influence on the powers-that-be that intrude on them is a hallmark of a socialist society, then the law remains very much a no-go area for the majority of the citizenry in capitalist Britain. Since 1980 the number of people entitled to legal aid has fallen by 14 million. A decade ago, nearly 80 per cent of the population qualified; now less than half meet the stringent income and wealth qualifications. A head of household on two-thirds average earnings with a wife and two children, who would have got free legal aid in 1979, now has to contribute 7 per cent of earnings. Access to justice is increasingly limited to the rich and the poor, with most of middle England excluded.

The quality of justice is also often flawed. It often takes too long to get legal aid – typically up to three months. If you obtain money or property as a result of the case, legal aid turns into a loan, not a grant, and paying the Legal Aid Board back causes particular resentment in divorce cases. Legal aid also offers least help where many citizens most need it – in the tribunals dealing with social security, employment and immigration problems. Despite legal aid costs to the state which now exceed £400 million a year, action in the courts is still often painfully slow and expensive.

Law centres offer free services to individuals and to local groups specialising in housing, welfare, employment and immigration which are either not covered by legal aid or where help is not offered by local law firms. But as non-profit-making units, their funding has been severely squeezed over the last decade. There are now only seven in the whole country funded centrally by the Lord Chancellor's department. The rest, about 55, are funded mostly by local authorities, but this can inhibit their work when they are involved so frequently, for example on behalf of council house tenants, in contesting issues against their local authorities. Lack of a structured national funding system means large parts of the country are left without access to these services.

Alongside law centres, a key role in the free provision of skilled and detailed advice about rights and liabilities over the whole range of government legislation is played by citizens advice bureaux. But they too are seriously under-funded. Only 300 out of 1,000 bureaux have full-time paid managers. While new problems like AIDS and the poll tax put extra pressure on already-stretched resources, poll tax capping in areas of greatest need squeezes their funding and even threatens closure. New types of activity, like modernising community care work, go unfunded.

Access to Justice for All

What is needed is a new legal services scheme which can provide enforceable legal rights for the whole population without a means test. By analogy, Beveridge argued that the state should guarantee a basic right to income within a universal scheme of social security. He proposed there should be no means test in the major areas of risk. By the same principle the state should ensure that 'basic legal rights' are available to all through the provision of a free non-means-tested legal service.

A system of 'basic legal rights' should cover the following main areas of social welfare law:

- criminal cases where liberty, livelihood or personal reputation is in jeopardy;

- housing disputes concerning rent or mortgage repayments, liability for repair and security of tenure for tenants, aid to resident landlords on rent limits or repair liability or recovery of possession, and claims over the habitability of homes;
- disputed claims and appeals in social security matters;
- help for any party in custody or care proceedings in domestic and family cases, and maintenance proceedings;
- help over employment protection rights;
- immigration issues over the right of entry, residence and work;
- aid to parents in educational disputes over school allocation or suitability of teaching.

In these categories of case, legal services should be available to all individuals as a right for *essential* help in enforcing basic legal entitlements. There would of course have to be some protection against cases being pursued to unreasonable extremes: a lawyer could for example refuse to take on a case if he thought there was no reasonable prospect of success or advantage (though equally the client should have a right of appeal to a review panel in such cases).

This approach has the great merit of avoiding a means test. For it is much better that public financial support should be based, not on lowness of income, but on the relative social importance of the rights in question. It is more logical to provide help to all citizens for particular types of problem than to provide blanket help to those people who are poor. The implementation of this scheme would therefore be taking a huge step towards achieving for the first time real equality before the law for *all* citizens irrespective of class, income or occupation. No other single measure perhaps offers such a quantum leap in giving people power to gain control over their own lives by being enabled to hold their own in the disputes with authority that regularly afflict their day-to-day existence.

Outside the area of 'basic legal rights' however would still lie most matters where the remedies sought involve financial gain. Issues concerning debt or contract, or claims in tort for damage to property or nuisance, would not be subject to free legal services for all. In order therefore to achieve equal rights in such cases for poorer people, the network of local legal centres established nationwide to deliver this new service, initially in the inner urban areas of all towns and cities with a population above, say, 100,000 persons, should provide free legal aid and advice on these matters too for those living in poorer districts in the inner cities.

The enforcement of 'basic legal rights', essentially a social provision designed to tackle social problems, requires a new breed of lawyer. If it is to operate smoothly and effectively and not deter potential users by financial hurdles – and here the NHS offers a model – it should not be based on a commercial fee-paying relationship between lawyer and client. What is needed is the development of the public salaried sector of the legal profession that already exists in embryonic form in the framework of law centres.

None of this means that private practice will not continue to play a vital role, even within the 'basic legal rights' heart of the new scheme. Equally individuals may wish to supplement the basic scheme by private insurance against particular risks or liabilities which fall outside the scope of the basic service. There is therefore no reason why a salaried service and private practice should not co-exist. While a new class of salaried lawyers, particularly younger entrants to the profession, may become the dominant providers of basic legal rights, there will still be a role for a private practitioner paid a retainer to deal with the service on a part-time basis, and in other areas private law firms may wish to accept work on a fee basis. There will therefore still be full freedom of choice for the client in the selection of a lawyer. The difference will be that high-quality legal aid and advice will no longer be confined to the fortuitousness of private wealth or means-test bureaucracies.

The proposed new legal scheme should be run by a legal services commission. This should be an independent corporation funded by the government, on similar lines to the UGC and the Arts Council, and accountable through a minister to parliament. It should have a broadly based, mainly lay membership. It would take over all the current functions of the Law Society and the courts in regard to legal aid, and would lay down guidelines to the review panels and lawyers. Its watchwords should be accountability, flexibility and commitment to equality of access to justice for all.

Taking Liberties with Civil Liberties

Providing equal access to legal services covering the main range
of social welfare is not however sufficient to ensure that all
citizens can pursue their lives freely and without hindrance.
While Britain is certainly not on a par with gross human rights
abusers in the Third World and cannot in any sense be properly
termed a police state, nevertheless serious breaches in civil
liberties and basic human rights are widespread in the UK, and
the lives and careers of perhaps a million or more citizens are
blighted, or at least threatened, in consequence.

Big Brother Encroachment

Interference with the freedom and privacy of citizens by the
security authorities – MI5, Special Branch, and the police – is
much more widespread than is generally realised. Telephone
taps, officially stated to number about 450 a year, were said by
Merlyn Rees in 1980 to number 2,000–3,000 every year when he
was home secretary. Unofficial estimates however put the
number at 30,000 a year ('Open File', *The Observer*, 30 October
1988). Even that is dwarfed by the potential of the new
computer-run telephone exchange, System X, which will allow
Tinkerbell (the name given to BT's tapping centre) to monitor
individual calls secretly and more easily without any legal
safeguards. Officially each tap requires a warrant from the home
secretary, who is not supposed to issue one unless he is reasonably
sure that it will lead to a conviction for a serious offence and that
other methods of investigation have been, or would be, unsuc-
cessful. In fact, that power has been delegated to senior home
office officials and senior police officers, and anyway MI5 and
GCHQ operate under a single blanket warrant. Known targets
have included trade unionists (for example Mick McGahey and
Ken Gill), sensitive pressure groups (for example Joan Ruddock
and John Cox of CND), strikers (for example Grunwick 1975, the
steel union ISTC 1982, and the NUM 1984), journalists and MPs.

The main organiser of this snooping is MI5. Ostensibly the role
of the security services (or secret police as they would be called
anywhere else) is spy-catching and counter-intelligence; in fact
these activities are relatively unimportant and its main function

is domestic political surveillance. It is thus the establishment's under-cover defence against the British left. Indeed its immense power rests principally on its freedom to decide who is the internal enemy and to use extra-legal methods wherever it chooses (as Peter Wright put it in 'Spycatcher': 'bugging and burgling their way all over London'). Its activities include influencing job selection in the whole public sector and in sensitive parts of the private sector, monitoring new political formations and the conduct of industrial disputes, and limiting the access of journalists and academics to official information.

Information is collected by MI5 on individual citizens on a vast scale. Its registry contains dossiers on over half a million people. But new computer capacity installed at its Mayfair headquarters in the early 1980s has a storage capacity to hold files on 20 million people, and is linked to a growing network of other government computer databanks (at the Inland Revenue, DSS, and Department of Employment). Ultimately this could become a comprehensive national filing system on each individual, with the linkage of personal files operated by the unique National Insurance number. How accurate this information is regarding any individual, or how it might be used, has never been subjected to any external check.

Information Used as a Weapon

Data on official computers, like the Police National Computer which has 40 million personal records, may be inaccurate, irrelevant, incomplete or out-of-date. The case of Jan Martin, documented by BBC *Panorama*, revealed that a completely unfounded suspicion that her husband, observed while travelling in Holland, might have been a member of the Baader Meinhof gang had not only been passed from the Dutch police to Scotland Yard, but had subsequently been transferred to a private industrial company, Taylor Woodrow, the employer of Mrs Martin who was promptly sacked without explanation. It was only because her father happened to be a former Scotland Yard inspector that the source of this extremely damaging rumour came to light. One wonders how many thousands of other people may suffer such discrimination, but never discover why.

The Economic League operates a nationwide private enterprise blacklisting service which vets commercial workers in the same way that MI5 vets civil servants and defence contractors for the government. More than 2,000 British firms secretly belong to the League, which keeps confidential files on nearly 250,000 workers. When anyone applies for a job, the company personnel officer secretly rings the League and gives a code number. The League clerks consult the index, and if a name appears, provide data accusing the individual either of trade union activity, links with Communist or Trotskyist groups, links with radical causes such as anti-apartheid, CND or women's lib, or with merely having taken part in a strike. The worker is then refused a job, often under the false pretext that a previous employer had found their work unsatisfactory. As a result, thousands are denied jobs either on political grounds which are a denial of a free society or on grounds of malicious tittle-tattle which even if untrue they can never disprove.

Altogether as many as 1 million public and private sector posts are subject to security vetting, most by a secret process concealed from job applicants, according to research published in 1990 by Civil Liberties Trust. Positive vetting covers 66,000 posts considered by the government to be sensitive, including jobs in the nuclear industry and British Telecom. A further 0.75–1 million job applicants are subject to negative vetting, which is covert, including junior posts in Whitehall departments and with defence contractors, builders working on government sites and nuclear plants, and some jobs in the BBC. It involves a trawl through MI5, Special Branch and police criminal records, using the 'nothing known against' procedure. Since applicants have no way of knowing if they have been denied a job because of information on these files, such vetting contravenes the European Convention on Human Rights because it provides no effective remedy for those secretly denied security clearance.

Official Harassment and Intimidation

The 1980s have witnessed the ideological and pragmatic assertion of a new power – the forces of law and order – obtruding ever more sharply and directly on the rights and freedoms of individual citizens. In part this is a reaction to wider forces in society, particularly the rising levels of crime, including violent crime and the big demo (Grunwick, the miners' strike and the poll tax riots). But partly also it reflects the dominant Thatcherite theme of popular authoritarianism, to which the demos are themselves a reaction.

Greater powers to restrict demonstrations and pickets were given to the police under the Public Order Act 1986. Seven days' notice of any demonstration has to be given to the police who now have the power to impose conditions. Also in 1986, the government started to issue chief constables with plastic bullets and CS gas, even if their police authorities did not want them. In 1988 the Thatcher government abolished the centuries-old right of the defence in criminal trials to 'peremptory challenge' of jurors, though the prosecution's right to do so was retained. They also decided to scrap the historic 'right of silence' under police interrogation in Northern Ireland as a prelude to its abolition on the mainland. The 1988 Security Services Act gave members of MI5 the legal right to bug and burgle people's homes, provided only that the home secretary has secretly authorised it. In addition, the 'temporary' Prevention of Terrorism Act has been repeatedly renewed, not because it increases prosecutions, but for information-gathering and for no-questions-asked deportation of unwanted Irish. Similarly, police stop-and-search powers have been used against tens of thousands over the last decade, though the numbers actually detained and later charged, or later still convicted, have been tiny.

These increased police powers have been matched by the latest law enforcement technology. Community policing has been replaced by fire brigade policing, the use of computerised command and control systems for the rapid deployment of force. Paramilitarist tactics were first used against the miners at Orgreave in 1985, then the printers at Wapping and the peace convoy at Stonehenge. The Association of Chief Police Officers (ACPO), in practice accountable to none but itself, has secured the adoption throughout the country of Tactical Support Units equipped with riot shields, vizors, plastic bullets, smoke grenades, tear gas and live firearms including sub-machine guns. We are indeed seeing the rise of a type of policing akin to that of an occupying army – the words of John Alderson, former chief constable of Devon and Cornwall.

Secrecy to Deny Rights and Power

Britain has the most censored media and the most secretive government of the Western democracies. The Official Secrets Act, passed by parliament in 30 minutes in 1911, contained the notorious catch-all section two which threw a ring fence round all government material, thus monopolising access to the power of decision-making to ministers and their officials, when perhaps 80 per cent of that material ought in a real democracy to be open to public debate. Now the amended Official Secrets Act 1989 has drawn the chains even tighter. Where a civil servant leaks what the government designates as sensitive information, there is no longer a defence either of public interest or of prior publication elsewhere, even if what is exposed is criminal, corrupt, fraudulent or even treacherous. So if MI5, our secret police, were to murder environmentalists and destroy their property (as the French secret service did to Greenpeace), or burn the offices and meeting places of anti-government groups (as the Canadian secret services did to Quebec separatists in 1972), or bug and burgle the political opposition (as Nixon did at Watergate), or send poison pen letters and hate mail to radicals (as the FBI did to Martin Luther King), nobody shall be permitted to know.

The outcome of the Spycatcher saga is that no intelligence agent can ever discuss his or her work, even if it is long out of date. This is not to defend the nation from its enemies, but (like the Securitate) to shield the government from its citizens. The Broadcasting Act 1990 allows the police to seize unseen background material to programmes. The broadcast ban on Sinn Fein and the UDA, passed in 1988 and unprecedented in recent history, continues. The government sent Special Branch officers in 1987 to raid BBC offices in Scotland to stop the broadcasting of its film on the spy satellite Zircon.

Another deeply disturbing dimension of secrecy in Britain which erodes the whole framework of equal rights under the law concerns the prevalence of freemasonry among the police and other groups in authority. While not necessarily embracing the octopoid corrupting entanglements like those of the Italian P2 masonic lodge (though the full truth is certainly not known), it has been estimated that up to one in five policemen may be freemasons (Martin Short, *Inside the Brotherhood*, 1988), including many in very senior positions. Many examples of law-breaking by freemasons have been cited, ranging from illegal checks on criminal records, through corrupt influence on career advancement, to stopping the Stalker inquiry into the alleged RUC shoot-to-kill policy in Northern Ireland.

Social Ostracism and Maltreatment

Britain remains a citadel of bigotry against minority groups, be they gypsies, the mentally ill, beggars, immigrants, homosexuals, prisoners, AIDS victims or whatever. Fanned by Thatcher's constant abuse of strikers, trade unionists, demonstrators and scroungers, her thinly veiled smear of blacks ('swamping' by an alien culture), social workers and the unemployed, and tabloid hysteria reinforcing the official line, the 1980s has seen an ugly rise in intolerance of dissent and erosion of fundamental rights. Section 28 of the 1987 Local Government Act, prohibiting local authorities from any promotion of homosexuality, symbolised the growing atmosphere of official persecution.

But it is not only attitudes of hostility to these groups that have hardened markedly in the 1980s. Physical abuse of these individuals by the forces of authority has become much more widespread. Strip searches and intimate body examination, used routinely in Northern Ireland, are now used frequently on the mainland both in prisons and police stations to humiliate persons marked down as troublesome. In line with more forceful and aggressive policing, beating up prisoners in custody, again both in prisons and police stations, has become more commonplace, even occasionally to the point where the prisoner dies. While torture as a routine administrative procedure in places of detention has never been true of Britain as of many Third World countries, nevertheless severe overcrowding, degrading conditions in cells, 23 hours per day lock-ups and an under-current of violence have produced a steadily rising suicide rate in prisons.

Civil Rights as Power to the Individual

Britain needs a civil and social rights revolution. One expression of this is the regular demand, most notably from the Charter 88 movement, that the European Convention on Human Rights should be enshrined in statute so that its articles are enforceable in the British courts. This has been resisted by the left on the grounds that the judiciary cannot be trusted to interpret such a Bill of Rights with fairness and impartiality. But that is the wrong response. The present judiciary may well be biased in their rendering of the law, but that is an argument, not for rejecting a sensible law they might abuse, but for radical changes in the recruitment and review of tenure of the judges. The real weakness of the European Convention is that, by itself, it is neither comprehensive nor explicit enough to reverse the current imbalance of power between the citizen and the state.

What is needed is an over-arching civil liberties charter covering all the known areas of abuse and opening up individuals' access to key public information and decisions on rights in every feasible context. The main principles of the charter, which should be vigorously promoted in a new published declaration of personal freedoms, should cover all the following issues of contention

Freedom of Information

The blanket use of spurious 'national security' allegations to suppress a public entitlement to know information of crucial public interest was finally exposed by the political prosecution of Sarah Tisdall and Clive Ponting in 1985, neither of whom it was ever suggested had actually endangered the security of the nation. The new Official Secrets Act 1989 actually tightened up the shroud of secrecy surrounding the government's 'specified categories' of information, imposing up to two years' imprisonment regardless of whether the disclosure was harmful.

While protecting all matters of genuine national security, it is way past time to repeal these official secrets acts, which at bottom line are about preserving the monopoly of power to ministers and senior officials. The presumption that everything is secret unless it is publicised by a government department or leaked by a minister should be replaced by the open principle that all information should be available unless there are specific reasons for its being withheld. On the American model, any citizen should therefore have the right to require to see official documents in all cases except those which the freedom of information registrar certifies are excluded by genuine and tightly drawn considerations of national security, commercial confidentiality, criminal apprehension or personal privacy.

Individuals' Right of Access to Records Held on Them

The proliferation of personal records about individuals can cause them considerable damage when those records are inaccurate, irrelevant or transferred to people who have no business to see them. In response to the European Convention on Automatic Data Processing, the government introduced the Data Protection Act in 1984. However, the act exempts manual records, qualifies the right of access of the data subject so that it is almost meaningless, and sets up an enforcement body so weak that it cannot police the measure effectively (20 staff to manage half a million registrations under the act).

Moreover there is currently no constraint on the official recording of pejorative information which could be misused with highly damaging effects. The chief constable of Yorkshire has stated that he would record as 'subversive' anyone with communist or extremist political views, homosexuals and 'anyone else who undermines marriage and the family', those who campaigned for shorter prison sentences for anti-social crime, people who tried to undermine discipline in schools and people who advocated the acceptance of certain drugs. Where a chief constable is so apparently oblivious of how such authoritarian and politically partisan procedures can seriously harm ordinary citizens, the case for closer protection of civil liberties is clearly made, especially when another chief constable (for Devon and Cornwall) found it necessary to destroy many of his Special Branch's records as irrelevant and malicious gossip.

The civil liberties charter should therefore guarantee to all citizens the right of access to official records held on them unless the data protection registrar certifies in a written statement that genuine issues of national security preclude it. In such cases he should, if requested, examine the file himself and report to the individual concerned whether it contained anything improper or irrelevant. In addition, formal regulations should be issued limiting the collection of information to what is strictly relevant for that purpose, protecting sensitive information like that relating to politics or religion, and giving the individual the right to legal redress and financial compensation where data is found to be stored about him which is irrelevant and pejorative.

The Right to Privacy

People have right to privacy in their homes, in their correspondence and in their family life, as Article 8 of the European Convention confirms. Yet this is repeatedly breached. The administrative authorisation of telephone tapping and interception was found to be an invasion of personal privacy in the case of Malone. The consequential Interception of Communications Act 1985 did not cover bugging and surveillance devices and failed to allow for prior judicial warrant before taps were introduced. In the future, the System X electronic telephone-exchange system, when it is completed in 2014, will mean that engineers need not even enter telephone exchanges and laboriously connect taps; the software can be re-programmed rapidly and at a distance.

The civil liberties charter should require that MI5, which has repeatedly been shown not to abide by their own guidelines (as set up in the Maxwell-Fyffe directive), be made accountable to parliament via a select committee of senior privy councillors. Where it can be shown that MI5 or Special Branch have breached approved guidelines outside the strict requirements of national security (with the select committee acting as final arbiters of the boundaries of this concept), then they should, like all other institutions, be answerable to the courts and any appropriate penalties levied. The fiction that MI5 does not exist, and is therefore not accountable at law, should be ended as the cover for the extra-legal sabotage against dissenters that it is.

Privacy in one's own home and family is vital for freedom in a civilised society. Legal protection of privacy has been recommended since the Younger Committee of 1972, and should now be actioned to outlaw electronic eavesdropping, bugging and burgling, or any other invasion of personal privacy of the private individual's home or family by the state security services, police, private investigators, journalists or any other snoopers. The only exceptions would be those cases specifically sanctioned either by the select committee of privy councillors for security purposes or by the home secretary personally for police surveillance purposes (for example in relation to drug money-laundering operations).

Protection Against Abuse of Police Power

While all law-abiding citizens want the police to have adequate powers to prevent and counter crime and to maintain peaceful public order, the 1980s have thrown up abundant evidence of the need for new protections against police excesses that grossly abuse individual rights. Several reforms are needed.

Both the Police and Criminal Evidence Act 1984 and the Public Order Act 1986, which significantly extend police powers at the expense of freedom of the citizen, should be substantially repealed. The former creates a new offence of riot with up to 19 years imprisonment, a new offence of criminal trespass, and a possible six-month offence for using offensive words. The latter gives police power to hold persons for up to four days without charge, allows for intimate body searches, and introduces new stop and search powers for use on the streets. A new codification of police public order powers should redress this repressive imbalance of state power against the citizen.

The use of violence against persons in custody in police stations, now far from uncommon, needs to be stamped out. A scheme allowing visits to police stations by a board of visitors at unannounced times should be introduced, with opportunities for any prisoner to give evidence to them in private if he has allegations to make. A similar system should operate in prisons. The code of conduct for police should make clear that any officer in serious breach of this rule would be liable to dismissal.

The complaints system against the police is flawed by the lack of independent inquiry: police officers investigate other police officers. A police complaints commissioner should be established, entirely independent of the police, with regional staffing sufficient to investigate all the most serious cases, particularly allegations of violence. Their decisions would be binding, with appeal to the courts only on a point of law.

Prisoners' Rights

While those who have been sentenced to prison for an offence should make amends wherever possible for any wrong they have done, they should not be deprived of basic civil rights except those consequent on their imprisonment. Yet conditions in Britain's jails are so overcrowded and insanitary that they are widely held to be responsible for the high wave of suicides (179 in the four years 1987–90).

As Judge Tumim, chief inspector of prisons, recommended in his report in December 1990, there should be minimum standards for prisoners which they are clearly informed of and which are enforceable in the domestic courts. These should include a clean bed, sufficient living space, access to a toilet and wash basin at all times, a daily shower and reasonable privacy. Moreover, since the aim of imprisonment must be rehabilitation and not retribution, the regime should also include prison work at realistic levels of pay, not least to fund recompense to the victim, daily exercise, education and medical attention reaching the standards of the NHS.

Democratising the Media

There is another important area where civil rights are seriously compromised – the right to a reasonably impartial, or at least broadly balanced, flow of information about what is really going on in society. That is obstructed at present by the semi-monopoly concentration of power in mass communications. Nearly 85 per cent of all national daily and Sunday newspapers sold in the UK have been owned by three vast corporations dominated by individual tycoons (Murdoch, Stevens and Maxwell until his untimely death). In addition, 90 per cent of 'independent' local radio stations are linked by ownership to just three companies. The Tory Broadcasting Act 1989 is leading to even greater concentration of control in press, radio and television.

In a democratic society this offends the essential requirements of diversity, balance and access. It enables the fixing of the daily agenda of the nation (on which TV later feeds), the news selection of what should be given attention and what excluded, and the slanting of opinion formation to reflect the values and priorities of one dominant group which constantly identifies the national interest with its own social and ideological interests. There is no national newspaper which is really separate from the establishment. The long-term pervasive shaping of public stereotypes and attitudes in the hands of a very few, very rich men is a serious, if hidden, abuse of power in a supposedly open society – indeed it is more significant than the outrageous individual abuses regularly highlighted in the tabloid press.

Since in a decentralised and democratic society information is power, there are few public services more important than getting a media which is genuinely pluralistic, balanced and accountable, and accessible to all interests, not just the most powerful ones. How can that be secured?

To ensure real diversity, anti-monopoly legislation should be used to secure divestment of the current press empires so that no one owner owned more than one daily and one Sunday newspaper or more than 5 per cent of the equity in any radio or TV station. An Open Press Authority (OPA) should be appointed to oversee the transfer of ownership to other bodies, preferably to independent trusts (like the *Guardian*) or co-operatives. To assist the launch of new titles, especially regional and local, the OPA would be empowered to provide limited start-up capital in accordance with public guidelines reflecting the balance of voting opinion averaged over the two previous elections (as in Sweden). Other European experience has clearly shown that allocation of government aid through an independent intermediary according to predetermined publicly stated criteria does not in any way encroach on freedom of the press (which given the almost total domination by a handful of men scarcely exists in any genuine sense in Britain today anyway). Another means to extend diversity without giving rise to backdoor censorship by government would be by authorising the OPA to redistribute advertising revenue, again according to criteria publicly specified in advance. At present, how advertisers spend their budgets largely determines which newspapers are available for purchase.

To obtain balance and accountability, more is required than simply changing the structure of the press. A right of reply should be instituted, as already exists in France, Germany and Denmark. Where a newspaper (or radio or TV programme, though they are already covered by a legal duty to be impartial) has carried a factually inaccurate or grossly distorted report concerning an individual or organisation, the latter should have a legal right, subject to their proving their case before a tribunal, to a reply made available free of charge and of equal length to, and in the same position as, the original article within three days or, where challenged by the newspaper or radio or TV, within seven days at most. Also a media commission with statutory powers should replace the present voluntary and ineffective Press Council, and should issue a detailed press and broadcasting code to reflect the highest standards of public interest publishing and broadcasting. It should then employ staff for systematic monitoring of media content against these standards, and publish the results, with powers to fine owners for serious or repeated offences.

Democratising access to the media requires a more radical solution, one that opens up further the pioneering work of activists in community access broadcasting. It is one thing to ensure that they, the newspaper proprietors and broadcasters when they communicate with us, offer a genuine choice of article and observe fair play in their presentations. It is another to allow us, members of the public, the power to use the technologies of mass communication to inform and debate with each other. But that is what decentralising control over the instruments of modern communications really means. For this purpose therefore a positive right should be instituted, subject to minimum criteria of appropriateness, for interest groups of all types and opinions to have access to radio, press and television to make a presentation and to argue their case. Of course the media commission would have to regulate this new avenue of expression so as not to undermine the general function of the media to entertain and inform, but for the first time the rich diversity of latent talent, hidden culture and suppressed interests would be accorded an effective and equal voice.

In summary, part of a socialist society empowering people to gain control over their own lives must involve a framework of rights and structures to enable individuals effectively to protect themselves against oppression or harassment by those in authority in any sphere. A system of basic legal rights, giving free access to the law in all key areas of social welfare, plus a new comprehensive civil liberties charter detailing specific enforceable powers for individuals to assert their rights and seek redress in all main areas of contention with public authorities, offer such a framework which can dynamically rectify the current imbalance of power between the individual and the state in secretive and authoritarian Britain.

8

Getting the Public Services
People Need

Many public services are, and are perceived to be, monolithic, bureaucratic and inflexible. If people are to have the power to determine their own lives as they would wish, then they require services to be responsive, accountable and adaptive. They also want services that are innovative so as to accommodate, or even anticipate, changing needs.

The Problem

Most public services are accountable to the population they serve primarily through the local ballot box. This is a blunt and ineffective channel of accountability for several reasons. Votes for local councillors, or for one party rather than another, do not connect with specific complaints about any particular local service. Notoriously, swings in local government elections are overwhelmingly a function of the popularity or otherwise of central government at that moment, which swamps any fine-tuned perception of local council performance. And the quality of local councillors, who are in theory ultimately responsible for the management of local public services, is in general too low. They are too little trained and too motivated by concern with local status, to exercise real professional control over staff handling, monitoring of performance, service delivery or innovation in techniques.

Thatcher addressed this question by seeking to introduce a new means of accountability via the market. It was designed to maximise individual choice unencumbered by local bureaucracy and took several forms. In the NHS it was hospital opt-outs and GP cash-limited budgets. In education it was school opt-outs and student loans. In housing it was the selling-off of municipal estates. In social security it was the cash-limiting of the remedying of poverty by the Social Fund. In local government generally it was the poll tax. But the market model was rapidly seen to have major defects. It led to very large numbers of people clearly in need having to go without (for example those rejected by the Social Fund). It polarised services between concentration of resources in some favoured locations and sink-holes in surrounding areas. It twisted democratic choice in the interests of ulterior ends (for example in the Torbay Council housing estate sell-off, all abstainers were counted as being in favour). It undermined the rational allocation of resources in meeting need both at national and local levels. And by squeezing budgets in the internal market within the public sector, it favoured the rich and well-off who could supplement or replace an enfeebled state system by private provision.

A new model for service delivery is therefore needed. It should discriminate neither for nor against either the public or private sectors, but use whichever maximises accountability for the individual, without regard to income, and for all equally. It should aim for direct rather than indirect accountability to the public wherever possible. Whatever channels of control are used, they should be open freely and equally to all, and not be biased in favour of one section of the population rather than another. They should be pro-active, and seek to maximise individuals' power to influence both service planning and performance. They should be effective in meeting complaints and securing genuine redress of grievances.

Giving Individuals Power Over Local Services

Such a model should be deployed to fit the particular structure of each major local service. In the case of housing, municipal tenants should have the right to self-management. They should be encouraged and trained to exercise the various responsibilities involved, and the adoption of each successive layer of increased executive authority should be triggered by a ballot of all the tenants concerned. Initially, such questions as landscaping and communal facilities might be taken over, then repairs and maintenance matters, and finally rent collection and new investment. As each further responsibility was taken on, the elected tenants' association would be allocated the same budget as that provided by the council for the purpose, with future annual budgets negotiated with the council until rent collection made the association self-funding. In that way council tenants would steadily assume control over their own living area, even if they did not individually have the financial power to gain independence through the market.

For the health service the aim should be the maximum involvement of the public in the strategic planning and delivery of services, while leaving medical and technical matters to the professional staff. One obvious mechanism is directly elected district health authorities, removing a political patronage ruthlessly exploited by the Tories. Budgets would then be determined centrally, but allocated locally and directed to local priorities by persons directly accountable to the local community. Another is that GPs should be required to issue a 'practice statement' setting out full details of services provided at each health centre, surgery and clinic in the area, giving patients more choice and the opportunity to be consulted about surgery times, preventive check-ups for women and wider community care. A patients' charter should be instituted, guaranteeing that each health authority will make available a full range of services, that full information will be given when requested about an individual's own medical condition and proposed treatment, that access will be provided to medical records and that a right is given to a second medical opinion.

Social security offices, now often run with the humiliating indignity of a cattle market, should be civilised by being put under a supervisory board made up of at least 50 per cent claimants or their chosen representatives. The manager would then be the chief executive responsible to the board for day-to-day operational management of the office, while the board would be responsible for policy on the functional handling of the work of the office, though not for benefits or finance which would continue to be settled by government. The members of the board would include at least one representative elected by long-term claimants from each of the main claimant groups – the elderly, the disabled, the unemployed, the homeless and lone parents. Elections would be organised from each DSS office on an annual cycle.

In addition, as an index of consumer satisfaction or grievance with the service locally provided by DSS, there should be annual consultative meetings held at the DSS offices or other appropriate premises to which each main group of claimants are invited for a frank exchange with local staff about the quality of the service and how it might be improved. Requests made by consumers which went beyond the purview of local management – for example that there should be sufficient staff to explain complexities of the benefit structure, to ensure that full entitlement was acquired and to advise on transition to the labour market wherever that could be achieved – should be passed in detail to the policy-makers at DSS headquarters.

Education should be based on much closer school–community links since research has repeatedly shown that what happens to the child in the family environment outside school is just as important educationally as what happens in school. Parents should form, by election, three-quarters of the membership of the board of governors – thus taking a relationship with the head teacher similar to that proposed above for the board of social security offices with the manager. Home–school contracts should make clear that an integral part of teachers' duties centre round their relationships with parents of their pupils, particularly those requiring remedial support, and that regular appraisals of their tenure will include this as an important element. Parental opinion of their children's teachers will thus be sought as part of the assessment of their performance. Insofar as education is rightly seen, not simply as an intellectual process, but more broadly as a process of physical, aesthetic, emotional and moral/spiritual development, parents and others in the local community clearly have a key role to play. In consultation with teachers and governors they should be closely involved in enhancing the overall development of their pupils both in the classroom and outside.

Re-appointments to Reflect Accountability

Senior public service posts are at present filled usually internally within the system rather than through some external filter of approval. Judges are dependent on the patronage of the Lord Chancellor. Magistrates are appointed on the basis of recommendations (or vetoes) of a secret local advisory committee reporting to the Lord Chancellor's department. Chief constables are appointed by the Home Office in consultation with ACPO. Managers of DSS offices, or of the new 1991 District Management Units, are appointed within the department. Permanent secretaries and other top civil service appointees are selected on the recommendation of a committee of existing permanent secretaries convened for the purpose, subject to ratification by the prime minister.

In no case is the public involved in any of these appointments, nor is there any appraisal later of continued tenure, and certainly not by the public who are the consumers or recipients of the services meted out. Yet there is abundant recent evidence which suggests this is a serious omission. For example, judges who have half-excused or given minimal sentences for rape, or who handed out a prison sentence to a woman who refused out of fear to give evidence against a violent boyfriend (Judge Pickles), or who negligently (or wilfully) misconstrued or ignored clear evidence exculpating victims subsequently subjected to long prison terms (the Guildford Four and Birmingham Six) – all of which have scandalised the public – are not at present liable to be publicly brought to book. Certain magistrates who notoriously display class bias in what passes for summary justice cannot at present be later held to account. Chief constables with highly controversial records (for example Anderton in Manchester and Oxford on Merseyside) know that their jobs are safe and that they will not have to answer for their actions in any public forum. Managers of DSS offices and directors of local authority departments, especially housing, experience no comeback at present however rude or offensive their staff may be in dealing with members of the public.

What is therefore needed is a re-appraisal of tenure at regular intervals (perhaps every five or seven years) for all persons holding strategic positions of authority in all major public services. Labour MPs are subject to re-selection by their constituency parties between five-yearly general elections, and arguably nobody in senior positions in public life should enjoy indefinite tenure without regular independent assessment of performance. So far as feasible, that re-appraisal should involve members of the public, whether directly or indirectly.

Local service providers like DSS managers, directors of housing, directors of education, directors of planning departments, and other top managers in local government, having been appointed as now within the civil service or by local councillors, should be re-endorsed in post (or otherwise) by an electorate consisting of those members of the public who have been clients of the service over the previous five years.

Judges should be appointed, openly on the basis of published criteria, by an independent judicial commission whose membership should be balanced and subject to approval by the Commons select committee shadowing the Lord Chancellor's department. The current bias in favour of white, male and middle-aged judges should thus be progressively eliminated. The same commission should also review tenure at regular intervals of five or seven years, taking into account evidence as to performance provided by monitoring organisations or members of the public. Regional branches of the independent judicial commission should also be appointed which would perform the same functions in respect of magistrates.

In the case of top-ranking police officers, an independent police commission should similarly be established, to shift power away from the over-cosy relationship between ACPO and the Home Office and to open up tenure re-appraisals to public influence. Again, the membership of this commission would have to pass muster with the Commons Home Affairs Select Committee both for balance and width of representation, and would have a duty to consider evidence from affected members of the public as well as relevant organisations in deciding on re-appointments.

Civil service posts should be limited term contracts rather than protected for an indefinite period. At lower levels this requires regular review by senior officials of junior staff. At top level, it means that permanent secretaries at the peak of Whitehall departments should not be appointed by a cosy internal committee of existing permanent secretaries. The public should be fully involved in what are clearly strategic appointments via their own elected representative, the secretary of state for that department. He should sit with the official head of the civil service, the minister with responsibility for the civil service under the PM, and other permanent secretaries in related departments in choosing his own permanent secretary. The selection committee should seek to be unanimous, but no appointment should be made without the agreement of the secretary of state as the political representative of the electorate. Equally, a re-appraisal of tenure should be carried out at five or seven yearly intervals by a similarly constituted committee, but again no top official should remain in his existing post in that department if he did not command the confidence of his secretary of state. Such a system could be expected to make the great public bureaucracies much more responsive to the popular will.

Making Complaints Effective

Complaints procedures at present are generally little more than gestures by entrenched professional and industrial interests. They place very little power at the disposal of the members of the public who are complaining. That can, and should, be changed.

At present, if one makes a complaint against the police for harassment, corruption or violence, it is investigated by another police officer from another force. Without in any way impugning the integrity of individual investigating officers, it is clearly not an independent examination of the facts and the pressure on officers to protect their own cannot be excluded. If one complains about a doctor's treatment or a hospital procedure, the matter may go to the Health Service Ombudsman, but he is precluded from dealing with any issues that involve clinical judgement. If one complains about the handling of a case by a lawyer, the matter is normally referred to the Law Society which is more a trade union for solicitors than a channel of effective redress for aggrieved clients. If one is dissatisfied with the quality of service provided by the local housing, education or planning department, or by the local DSS office, or by the local MP, or by the local utility services of gas. electricity or telephone, there is really no effective complaints procedure at all.

The requirements of a proper complaints procedure are that it should be easily operated, at low cost or no cost, by an aggrieved member of the public, that it should be independent of the service complained of, and that it should be prompt without unreasonable delays. Above all it should be effective so that redress and satisfaction is quickly given, or if not, there are sanctions which can be brought to bear by the complainant, at least in serious cases. Only if all these conditions are met is there a real transfer of power from service providers to consumers.

The prototype model to meet these conditions should be an independent ombudsman constituted to meet the different requirements of each service. The police ombudsman should have a central staff to deal with the most serious complaints, and a regional staff to handle the less serious cases and those that can be settled by conciliation. His or her conclusions – whether the award of compensation, the requirement of an apology, dismissal of the complaint or whatever – would carry the force of law, and would be appealable against only if the judgement appeared to breach existing law. A legal ombudsman, dealing with complaints against lawyers, should have a staff structure modelled on his police counterpart.

The NHS ombudsman should no longer be precluded from dealing with matters that involve clinical judgement. The recommendation to deal with this made by the Davies Committee as long ago as 1973 should be implemented whereby investigation panels contain both medical and non-medical members. The principle of no-fault compensation should be adopted on the Australian and New Zealand models, with a Compensation Board not bound to apply the strict legal test of causation. The local government ombudsman, dealing particularly with housing, planning and social services complaints, should have his brief extended beyond maladministration, as now, to neglect of statutory duties and gross incompetence. He should not only be empowered to award compensation to an aggrieved elector, but also to require the local authority to act (or not to act) in a particular way – unless the local authority could demonstrate to his satisfaction that it did not have the funds to do so.

The social security ombudsman should have the power to require DSS to compensate a claimant for unduly late payment of benefit or time-wasting incompetence, as well as publicly reprimand it for inefficiency, excessive bureaucracy or staff incivility. He should also recommend both policy and procedure designed to improve the welfare of clients. A local utilities ombudsman, dealing with complaints about electricity, gas and telephone services, should have similar powers.

Each ombudsman should produce an annual report analysing

the type and nature of complaints received from the public in the previous year, and comparing it with previous years and with performance in other areas. The conclusions should be given wide publicity in the local and national media, and there should be at least one public meeting a year open to all local citizens to discuss the quality of service provided in the light of complaints received and how the service could be improved. In addition, a statement of all complaints received and investigated in the course of the year, with the names of complainants included where this is agreed by them, should be made publicly available. The statement should include in each case the response of the service provider and the action taken by the ombudsman.

Ensuring Minimum Standards and Promoting Best Quality

The Tory government has used competitive tendering or privatisation, or the threat of it, as a means of exerting pressure to improve standards. The drawbacks of this approach are now apparent. Cut-price tendering is often at the expense of quality; complaints about inefficiency or specific failures of performance can only be rectified by sacking the contractor and starting the tendering cycle all over again; and any reduction in cost is often secured not by improving the quality of the service, but by undercutting the terms and conditions of the employees.

A new framework is needed in which a quality culture can thrive. The basic requirement must be that residents receive customer contracts setting out the standard of service to expect for each main service. It should include details of when and how the service will be delivered, meaningful figures on how much the service costs, what to do and who to contact if things go wrong, and a firm timetable and procedure for dealing with complaints and, where appropriate, paying compensation. New powers vested in the hands of the public designed to give them effective control over local services would therefore include a service contract guaranteeing minimum standards, a right to compensation if these terms are breached, appeal to the relevant ombudsman to redress specific complaints, and as a last resort where poor performance persists, voting out the director of the local service at the end of his five-year term.

Other innovations are also needed to improve quality. Senior managers should be expected to spend time doing front-line jobs, like delivering meals-on-wheels or working on reception desks, so that they get a feel on the ground for what is delivered and how it is perceived. Quality audits involving professionals, managers and consumer representatives should regularly assess the quality and effectiveness of local services, and their reports should be published in full. A quality commission should establish a modest budget to make grants to help pilot new forms of service provision.

One new area where the principle of a minimum service contract should operate is residential and custodial institutions. In the case of the former – residential homes, mental handicap and psychiatric hospitals – the service contract should be handed to the resident on entry, or if he or she is not capable, it should be vested in an advocate or representative, whether a relative, friend or guardian ad litem, who takes responsibility for overseeing the care of the person concerned.

In the case of the latter – prisons, borstals and remand centres – the detained person would be handed on arrival a contract listing both his responsibilities and rights within a national system of accredited standards applying to that place of custody. If prison is to be a place of rehabilitation rather than retribution, the contract should include access to pay-phones, abolition of most letter censors, visiting rights (including occasional conjugal rights) of at least two a month, the right to wear your own shoes and clothes, more home leave whenever appropriate and a proper toilet system for each cell with an end to slopping out, as well as – at a different level – group therapy, individual counselling, the provision of meaningful work, and education. It should also immediately end gratuitous humiliations like strip-searching, unless sanctioned by a ministerial warrant for specific stated reasons. Enforcement of these rights for prisoners would be either via the courts for breach of contract or by appeal to a prison ombudsman or his regional staff.

There are at least two other important applications of the principle of enforcing minimum standards and promoting Quality Street services (or products). One is implementing what are called 'class actions'. At present, if a claimant wins a case against DSS at a tribunal, the gain is confined to him or her, even if there are thousands of others in an identical position. They must all make their own separate individual claims if they are to gain. Under a class action system, on the other hand, a gain made by one person would automatically apply to all other persons who are in an identical situation in respect of the issue before the tribunal. Introducing such a principle would ensure that better standards achieved anywhere in the system would immediately be universalised throughout it.

Another means of empowering people in terms of consumer standards lies through determined enforcement of product liability. At present the Consumer Protection Act excludes food and sets a weaker standard for product liability than elsewhere in the EEC. Strict liability should therefore be enforced so that consumers who are saddled with defective goods do not have to prove that the company was negligent. Equally, no fault compensation (that is without having to prove causal responsibility) should apply to the victims of medical accidents, transport accidents, injuries at leisure and entertainment facilities, as well as those damaged through infected food or unsafe consumer products. Arbitration schemes should be set in place to judge complaints and small-claims court procedures should also be promoted so that grievances can be settled, with replacement or money-back options, quickly and relatively costlessly.

Empowering the Poorest to Get the Services They Need

Clearly it is those on the lowest incomes who find it most difficult to secure the type and quality of services they want. This is for three reasons: they do not have the income to command the quality services they need from the private sector, public sector services are normally provided in kind without choice, and there is little or no comeback if public services are not up to standard. The last two sections of this chapter (pp 96–100) are designed to deal with the third problem. The other two require further reforms.

The principle of establishing a basic minimum standard of living below which no citizen should fall was one of the foundations of the post-war welfare state. It was flawed however in two respects. The level chosen in 1946 was not empirically based; it was derived by an inappropriate inflation yardstick from Poor Law minimum standards in 1938 which themselves had never been checked against reality since Seebohm Rowntree made his famous study of poverty in York in 1899. Now poverty is a relative concept, as even Adam Smith in *The Wealth of Nations* admits: 'By necessaries I understand, not only the commodities which are indispensably necessary for the support of life, but whatever the custom of the country renders it indecent for creditable people, even of the lowest order, to be without.' If that is so, there should be regular checks that society's basic living standard does make affordable those necessary things which custom requires 'creditable people, even of the lowest order', to have.

A century after Rowntree, an official Committee of Inquiry should now be urgently set up to establish what that principle means in the 1990s. It might be expected to include not only enough food to maintain healthy life, including three meals a day for children, but heating to warm all the living areas of the home if it is cold, a damp-proof home, beds for everyone in the household, enough bedrooms for every child over ten of different sex to have his/her own bedroom, a refrigerator, washing machine, telephone, two pairs of all-weather shoes and a warm waterproof coat for each person and toys for children. If that is what custom dictates, there is no way all those items could be purchased within the income support standard which stood in 1992 at £42.45 a week for a single adult and £66.60 a week for an adult couple. A new, higher standard therefore urgently needs to be drawn. If all such necessary resources and decent services are to be afforded, the standard might well have to be set up to 50–100 per cent higher.

The second flaw in the principle is that the Thatcher and Major governments breached it. Not only are deductions made for electricity and gas arrears and for rent and water charge arrears, but they added major new deductions for 20 per cent of the poll tax, Social Fund loan repayments, child maintenance from unemployed fathers and payments of fines if claimants commit an offence. As a result, by 1991 some 1.5 million persons had been forced below the Income Support line which was supposed to be society's irreducible minimum. This has simply created a vicious spiral downwards into deeper poverty and debt. The unequivocal principle should therefore be re-established that whatever living standard society fixes as the basic minimum for all citizens should be unwaveringly adhered to by government.

But getting the services that people want is only partly a matter of being firmly assured of adequate income. It is also partly a matter of how those services are delivered. At present, most household services for those on very low incomes, for example home helps, meals on wheels or domiciliary care, are delivered in a set form without variety or choice. A different model should be used which gives power to the otherwise helpless consumer to choose what *he or she* wants, which is not necessarily what the statutory provider offers.

Instead of homogeneous provision, equivalent funding should be put at the disposal of the consumer/claimant – whether pensioner, disabled or even perhaps homeless or unemployed – who would then have the opportunity to buy in whatever service, or combination of services, suited their particular needs. Because persons in these deprived groups may often lack either the acumen or expertise in handling a budget for such a purpose, they should where necessary have allocated to them an advocate, or counsellor ad litem, who would advise on all the relevant options, discuss with the client the most desirable, and secure its purchase on the most favourable terms. Such a system would greatly increase the power of some of the most vulnerable members of society to exercise their will effectively over matters essential to their welfare.

In summary, just as micro-processor technology has transformed both the structure of industry and its employment patterns, so it is enforcing a radical re-orienting of traditional services in the direction of the consumer. The market model of privatising or commercialising those services has been seen to put quality at risk and to polarise service provision along wealth–poverty lines. What is needed is a whole range of new mechanisms which put power directly into the hands of the public over the service controllers, but which do not depend on the vagaries of income and are not limited by the tendency of markets to cream off the most lucrative consumers. The cascade of proposals advocated in this chapter according to these criteria are probably only the tip of the iceberg of potential measures to diffuse real power over local services into the hands of their users.

9

Pathways out of Discrimination and Disadvantage

The people who need most of all to gain control over their own lives are those with least power – the poorest, the discriminated against, the disadvantaged. The numbers in each of these categories, or all three, rose steadily through the 1980s. What is needed now is not simply additional funding to make their poverty or discrimination or disadvantage more tolerable – however justified that might be – but assistance to enable them to overcome it and regain their independence.

Enabling Poor People to Escape their Poverty

Poverty increased sharply during the 1980s for two main reasons. One is that the Thatcher government persistently cut back the real level of benefits below the rates and structures prevailing in 1979. Even on the government's own figures, this cumulative cutback had by 1992 reached the staggering level of £39 billion – not far short of the government's total revenues from North Sea oil over the same period or of the total asset sales revenues from all the privatisations throughout the 1980s. The second reason is that the conditions causing poverty – very low income in retirement, disability, unemployment, lone parenthood and very low wages in employment – all increased during the decade.

Overall the number of persons dependent for one or more of these reasons on supplementary benefit/income support grew by 55 per cent to 8,910,000 in the period 1979–85. Those forced down to the poverty line through unemployment increased by 260 per cent, through lone parenthood by 60 per cent, and through disability by 36 per cent. The figures after 1985 are not known because the government deliberately changed the method of calculation after that date in order to preclude any comparison between the first and second halves of the 1980s. However, it is virtually certain that there has been a further significant growth in the numbers living at poverty level since 1985, and by 1991 the total had almost certainly passed 10 million, that is more than one in six of the whole population.

Yet poverty is not simply or even primarily the possession of too little money below a traditional but arbitrarily defined line. It is rather the benchmark of divided Britain that separates off those individuals, that large segment of the population, who are excluded from opportunities available to others. They are the victims of a disabling society, when what is needed is an *enabling* society that is comprehensive in its embrace. Poverty is not a mere static concept of an under-class defined by lack of resources. It is the dynamic consequence of discrimination which governs not only social life-styles, but the availability of economic opportunity. The remedy lies in opening up avenues of participation that are at present shut off and unlocking economic options which are presently closed.

Job Opportunities for the Over-60 Year Olds

A major cause of poverty is retirement, when the single person's pension (£52 a week from April 1991) is less than one-sixth of the national average wage (about £320 a week at April 1991). As a result some 3 million pensioners, nearly a third of the total, live on the income support poverty line. It is true that a gradually increasing proportion of retired persons also enjoy an occupational pension, but the average size of that is still small – only about £23 a week.

Earnings are clearly a major potential source for supplementing the incomes of older people. Yet they have markedly declined over the last 15 years. In 1974 their earnings amounted on average to nearly one-third of the basic pension, but by 1987 this had halved to only one-sixth. Even the government's abolition in 1989 of the earnings rule, whereby pensioners earning more than £75 a week and working over 12 hours a week had their state pension reduced £ for £ for earnings over this limit, made little difference. Still only some 13 per cent of pensioners continue to work after state pension age.

Obviously other measures are needed if older people are to have fully the job opportunities they may wish. The most important is greater flexibility over retirement age. Clearly many older workers in chronic ill-health by their mid-fifties are ready for retirement, while many other people in their late sixties or seventies or even eighties are physically fit and both able and wanting to hold down a job. We need a flexible decade (or double-decade, age 55–75) of retirement which accommodates much more closely to individuals' different needs and aspirations.

One alternative therefore would be to institute the option of part-employment/part-pension for older workers over 60 – though if all men aged 60 simply opted for retirement, the cost at maximum could be up to £3 billion a year, so the change would have to be phased in over time, say five years. It would end the principle of a pension as dependent on retirement, but the abolition of the earnings rule already points to this. Many of the younger elderly, especially among the 1.1 million people of pensionable age living *below* the income support line, let alone the further 2 million living *on* this poverty line, would for the first time obtain a ladder out of their poverty.

A better alternative would be to establish the minimum period actuarially required to purchase the state retirement pension (slightly over 40 years), and then allow individuals both to decide the start of their working life and the timing of its conclusion, whether at the minimum 40+ years later or whenever they wish thereafter. This would open up choice to people in their sixties to continue to seek employment if they wanted, without an arbitrary retirement age, without inequality between men and women, and without loss of pension rights. It would also remedy the demographic gap whereby the number of young people entering the labour market sharply reduces by 23 per cent in the first half of the 1990s.

Two other reforms are needed to open up the job market for older people. One is a prohibition on employers against age discrimination in their recruitment policies. Another is that access to high-quality re-training should be as readily available to workers over 50 as to younger workers (which is not the case at present with the government's Employment Training scheme). There are thousands of skilled and experienced workers made redundant in their fifties who at present have virtually no hope of re-entering employment, but who retain valuable and scarce skills that the skill-starved UK economy can ill afford to lose.

Enabling Disabled People to Get Jobs

Many people with disabilities of working age are unemployed or under-employed, not because of their own incapacity, but because of lack of essential support. This includes local services such as appropriate transport and community care, adaptations for access to buildings, skills training and benefits which recognise the value of part-time work for the partly incapacitated. The statutory quota scheme for the employment of disabled people is almost wholly ignored even within the Department of Employment.

The government now admits that the total number of the disabled in Britain is some 6 million. Their position has been weakened by the abolition of Industrial Injuries benefit in 1981, the abolition of Disablement Benefit where disability is assessed at less than 15 per cent (that is 90 percent of cases), and the abolition of the Reduced Earnings Allowance in 1990. The latter is a weekly-paid cash sum available to all those who suffer a permanent reduction in earnings caused by industrial injury or disease. There could scarcely be any greater deterrent to enabling disabled people to obtain or keep a job than removing this allowance.

In addition to restoring a partial incapacity benefit, other support services are needed. One is a realistic level of income support disregard (say £15 a week) to ease the transition from benefit to earnings. Another is a disability costs allowance which will provide assistance with the extra costs of disability matched to the degree of disability. The gross cost of the scheme would be high (up to £3 billion a year, so it would have to be phased in), but it would be substantially reduced by savings on income support and other means-tested benefits and by replacing other existing disability benefits.

More important however to maximise job entry for disabled people is much improved access to transport and buildings as well as full and free availability of training. Grants for buildings and rail/bus adaptation must be much more readily provided.

Apart from securing the basic participation of disabled people as citizens, front-end capital loading will rapidly be outweighed by long-term savings on benefits. The false economy in the drastic cut in the number of disablement resettlement officers must be reversed, as well as their abandonment of any pretension of enforcing the quota. A major new anti-discrimination law regarding disability should be incorporated in a new Bill of Employment Rights. And new technology training for the disabled, more integrated patterns of sheltered work, and such specialised services as Pathway should be greatly expanded. Not only will this put power for the first time into the hands of thousands of disabled people, it will also steadily close the unemployment gap between the current rate of 8 per cent for the non-disabled versus 26 per cent for the disabled – a major cause of their poverty.

Enabling the Unemployed to Get Work

The government's doctored statistics on the dole state there were already 2.8 million unemployed by mid 1992, though it is widely understood the true figure is over 3 million. Given that the last recession in 1979–81 drove unemployment up to 3.2 million in 1986, it is likely that the equally harsh recession of 1990–2 will push up unemployment again to the 3–3.5 million level. Equally the more than tripling of the numbers of people forced on to or below the poverty line by rising unemployment between 1979–85 is likely to be repeated in the first half of the 1990s. The relative value of basic unemployment benefit was halved over the Thatcherite decade, from 40 per cent of average weekly earnings in 1979 to only 18 per cent in 1990.

Two fundamental policies are required to overcome unemployment. One is a sustainable (that is, low inflation) economic growth policy, with a strong regional component, which has the reduction of unemployment as a central goal, not a residual after other priorities. The other is the steady systematic implementation of high-quality training schemes throughout the economy in place of the notoriously deficient YTS and ET schemes. This should include a new four-year traineeship for young people aged 16–19, embracing both academic studies and vocational training in modular form, and a statutory right to opportunity training for all adults, both for workers and the workless. There is perhaps no other mechanism which can so effectively empower people to gain control over their own lives as enabling them regularly and cumulatively to enhance existing skills or develop new skills whether in the same industrial sector or any different one as economic circumstances change.

Of course big improvements in both the quantity and quality of training are a costly investment. Against that however must be measured the cost of unemployment, if unremedied, which at its height in 1986 amounted in both benefits paid and taxes foregone to more than £20 billion a year. In fact we have fallen so far behind that economic competitiveness leaves us with no alternative but to make the necessary investment in full. But the net cost could be much lower over a five to ten-year period. For the precedents of the German training model and the Swedish Labour Market Board show high public and private investment in well-directed training can both speed up the return to work and keep unemployment levels well below the international average.

New imaginative measures are also needed to restore confidence and opportunity to the long-term unemployed in their approach to the job market, especially since surveys have shown that the longer they have been out of work, the more resistant employers are to recruiting them. In-depth counselling on an individual basis is clearly required for many who have been longest on the dole (though that is not to be confused with the current role of claimant adviser which has been perverted by the government into the function of benefit policing). A significantly bigger benefit disregard than the present derisory £4 a week (say £15 a week) would help many long-term unemployed to regain work disciplines through part-time employment. And if the unemployed are to acquire some real power to exercise initiative, the Enterprise Allowance should be restructured to allow a group of unemployed persons, as opposed to a single individual, to launch a co-operative venture with the support of technical and managerial aid from a regional or local CDA resource centre.

Getting Lone Parents out of the Poverty Trap

Lone parenthood has rapidly increased as a cause of poverty over the last decade. The latest official figures reveal that in 1985 some 1.6 million adults and children were living in lone-parent families on the poverty line. That involved about 70 per cent of all lone parents at that time. By comparison, only 19 per cent of two-parent families with children were driven down to this income level. The Family Expenditure Survey shows that the average gross household income of lone parents is less than half the average for all households and barely a third of that for couples with two children.

As a means of escape from poverty, a job is usually essential for a lone parent. Yet lone mothers are much less able to do part-time work than married women because without the support of a spouse income or maintenance they cannot afford to do so, not least because of the cost of child care. The government has actually made their plight worse. It did recently increase the earnings disregard (that is, what the mother can earn without loss of Income Support) from £12 to £15 a week so that a few more lone parents could be encouraged to go back to work. But then at the same time it stopped them offsetting the cost of child care against the family credit they could claim if they went out to work, so that most lone parents ended up worse off and were forced out of work back into dependency. The government also ruled that ET childcare allowances for trainees with under-school-age children should be restricted to the few who could claim as unemployed rather than as lone mothers. And if lone parents, avoiding both these traps, seek further education rather than ET, they can be subject to the DSS 21-hour rule (i.e. they cannot get benefit if their training is for 21 hours a week or more) as if they were unemployed.

Two key measures are needed to assist more lone parents to obtain work. One is to unpick the disincentive involved in the social security system's poverty trap for lone parents. It is absurd, for example, that unemployed people on income support have their mortgage interest payments covered, but if they go back to work and get family credit instead (as many lone parents do), they lose that help.

A second key requirement is a major national effort to increase childcare facilities. A statutory duty should be placed on all local authorities to provide comprehensive, integrated childcare services for the under-5s and 5–14 year olds out of school hours. Central government should encourage partnerships between local authorities, employers and voluntary agencies, where appropriate, to provide a choice of high-quality, secure childcare provision free or at low cost for pre-school or out-of-school needs.

This national investment would transform the job prospects for millions of mothers, and for lone mothers particularly would build a ladder out of the poverty from which at present they can rarely escape.

Ending the Powerlessness from too Low Wages

It is not only means-tested benefits that trap people in poverty. Extremely low wages – primarily, but by no means only, involving the 300,000 workers whose pay for full-time work is less than they would get in benefit if they were out of work – also produce powerlessness. Their pay is so low that it prevents their participating in a normal social life or making the economic contribution according to their potential.

Even though the number of full-time workers earning less than the Council of Europe's Decency Threshold (two-thirds of the average full-time wage) rose from 28 per cent in 1979 to 37 per cent by 1990, government economic policy throughout the same period continued to insist their wages were too *high*, not too low – that they had priced themselves out of jobs. But a Policy Studies Institute survey in 1990 found the opposite was true, that people made unemployed had generally worked in low-paid, low-skilled and manifestly insecure jobs, and even though they tended to come from low-paid jobs, they often went on to take a pay cut in their subsequent jobs. They were rendered almost permanently helpless in a job market over which they could get no leverage.

A decent basic wage is therefore a vital pathway out of poverty which puts a measure of power into the hands of the economically dispossessed. A national legal minimum hourly wage should be fixed, perhaps starting at 50 per cent of male median earnings (as proposed in chapter 5), which in 1991 represented £3.40 an hour, equivalent to £129 for a 38-hour week. Some 4 million very low-paid workers would gain from this new basic pay floor, though the economic power it would convey would still be modest. Over time as the state of the economy permitted, but within a 10–15-year timespan, the pay floor should be progressively raised as a proportion of earnings to two-thirds of the median male hourly rate.

This programme sets out a wholly new approach to the traditional problem of poverty. It does not deny (when the richest quarter of the population, according to the Inland Revenue, have *increased* their share of the nation's wealth in the decade to 1988 from 72 per cent to 75 per cent) that higher levels of benefit, and new kinds of benefit, are necessary – and affordable – if poverty is not to become an increasingly punitive and humiliating experience. But that is merely to alleviate the symptoms of the problem rather than to tackle its causes. The real solution is not paternalism towards those left entrenched in poverty, but extending them the power to make their own escape from their predicament.

Women: Emancipation Still Needed

Women, who are 52 per cent of the population and nearly 70 per cent of those in poverty, still, despite two decades of increasingly vociferous claims to equal rights, face serious discrimination. Women are treated differently from men in education, training, jobs and promotion. The law and social security both assume that married women are dependent on their husbands. Women are substantially under-represented in public life. Because they still take the main responsibility for looking after children or elderly relatives, most working women are forced into part-time low-paid jobs or cannot work at all, even if they wish to. In general, women are more likely to be poor, particularly in retirement. And few women escape the fear of violence, outside their home or even in it.

Getting Men Fully to Share Family Responsibilities

In order to gain control over their own lives, women need the liberation which can only flow from several major reforms. The first concerns family life. Nearly 7 million women are responsible for 12 million dependent children, with a partner or on their own. A fifth of women over 40 care for a sick or elderly relative. Mothers need help with childcare so that they can also have the opportunity to work, study and have some time for themselves. For this purpose all local councils should be required to provide comprehensive childcare services for the under-fives and out-of-school care for older children. To help women who have given up a job to look after an elderly relative, a new carers' benefit is needed which is related to the minimum wage, to replace the present Invalid Care Allowance at the derisory rate of £31 a week. Even more importantly, a full-scale programme of community care, based on a service contract spelling out what the local council should deliver, should include regular provision of respite care so that the carer, nearly always a woman, can still retain sufficient independence and not be engulfed by all-consuming duties.

Women can only make their full contribution at work if fundamental changes are set in hand at home, so that they can combine paid work with family responsibilities. That certainly includes allowing fathers to enjoy parental leave, career breaks and more flexible working hours, so that they have more time to care for their children. Employers should therefore be required to maximise these options for their male employees, following the introduction of a code of practice which sets out proposals for new patterns of working between the sexes.

Even a generation ago it was still customary for the man to go out to work while the woman stayed behind to keep house and look after the children. Now, however, when women make up 45 per cent of the workforce, it is becoming normal for a wife *both* to have a job, part-time or full-time, *and* to fulfil domestic and family responsibilities. Exclusive complementarity of roles between the sexes in the 1950s to 1960s is being rapidly replaced by overlapping roles in the 1980s to 1990s. Women will only become fully emancipated when men, culturally and as a matter of normal family convention, accept a combination of both work and domestic duties to match the same combination that women have already undertaken. The role of a radical government is to pave the way for that emancipation by using a range of pressures – statutory, fiscal and financial incentives – to influence male working patterns in the direction of a shared double role rather than an exclusive single one.

To assist that end, working families in Britain need the kind of support they get in other European countries. New mothers should be entitled to more maternity leave. Three months' parental leave should follow, which could be taken by the father. Fathers should have 10 days' paternity leave when the baby is born. Parents of young children should have the chance to take up to five family leave days each year.

Enforcing Equal Chances at Work

Women remain discriminated against at work in several ways – over pay, training, promotion and equal rights. Not only is this unfair to more than half the population, it also involves an under-employment of a huge reservoir of potential skills which Britain, with by far the worst-trained workforce among our main international competitors, cannot afford. Enabling women to take the power at work fully to match their abilities is a necessity for Britain as well as a long-delayed emancipation for themselves.

Women still earn on average, 20 years after the Equal Pay Act was passed, less than three-quarters of men's earnings. Women's average weekly earnings in 1990 were still £87 a week less than men's. This largely reflects women having received less training to enhance skills and enjoying less promotional opportunities. It reflects women workers being heavily concentrated in the poorest-paid jobs. Hence four out of five of those gaining from a national minimum wage pitched at 50 per cent of male median earnings will be women. But it does also mean that the principle of equal pay for work of equal value must be more effectively enforced by a new Wages Inspectorate.

The high-quality education and training that women need if they are to be empowered to develop their capabilities to the full should be provided by a new national curriculum (outlined in Chapter 4), new five-subject A-level courses, a new traineeship system for 16–19 year olds, and a new opportunity training scheme for adults. The former two would help girls mix science and technology with more traditional subjects – not only a widening of their horizons, but essential when Britain is so short of skilled professionals in areas like engineering, computing and science teaching. The four-year traineeships would enable young women for the first time to combine vocational and academic training of a high order, leading to proper qualifications and thence into highly-skilled and well-paid work. Opportunity training would enable older women, both those in and out of work or returning to work after caring for a family, to choose their own training course, financed by the local branch of Skills UK (the national training organisation), subject only to there being a demand for that skill with local employers and hence a job available at the end of the training contract.

While women will soon constitute half the workforce, they occupy nothing like half the positions of seniority in any area of working life. There are 10 males for every female in the higher civil service, 14 males for every female among partners in solicitor firms, and 25 males for every female on the judicial bench. There are no women in the cabinet, and a lower proportion of women in parliament than in all but 4 of the 21 states of the Council of Europe. When it comes to promotion, women face a glass ceiling, as several tribunal cases claiming sex discrimination have revealed (notably the charges brought by Alison Halford, assistant chief constable of Merseyside, against her boss in January 1991).

What is therefore needed is positive-action plans reflecting a code of conduct, for both industry and the professions, that in recruitment and promotion to higher-level posts women should be given preference over men, where they are equally qualified, if women are under-represented at that level in the area of appointment. As a measure of progress towards equality, employers should also be required (as under the Roudy law introduced in France in 1983) to submit a report on the relative position of male and female employees each year to the company council. The report would analyse, in each category of employment, the balance between men and women in terms of recruitment, pay, training, promotion, qualifications and conditions of work.

These measures together would progressively transform the position of women at work from one of subordination to one of equal power. They need to be complemented by a system of rights that enforce equal chances for women at work, whatever their situation. At present, half of all pregnant women in paid work in Britain do not qualify for the legal right to return to their job. In every other EEC country working women have the right to maternity leave. Almost half of all British women work part-time, more than in any other EEC country, yet are denied the same employment rights as full-time workers.

To redress this, a new charter for working women should include dependants' leave, flexi-week or flexi-year working arrangements, and full-time rights for part-timers and job sharers. All pregnant women in paid work should have job security. Employees returning to work after maternity or parental leave should have the option of working part-time with the same pro-rata rights and pay for up to five years, by agreement with their employer. Lone parents and those caring for chronically ill or disabled people should be entitled to extra leave. A framework of such rights would ensure that women carers, to the fullest degree feasible, were not forced to make a choice between their special responsibilities and keeping open opportunities at work.

Race: Breaking Down the Barriers of Exclusion

One other major group within the population who remain persistent victims of discrimination are black people. It is not just that very substantial numbers of black people remain excluded from mainstream economic life by virtue of long-term structural unemployment (rates of 13–14 per cent in 1987–9 when the rate for whites was 8 per cent). Even among those in work, the peripheral job sector – part-time, short-term, insecure – is increasingly filled by Third World workers, no longer settlers, but refugees. Hotel and catering workers, the contract cleaners in hospitals or airports, security guards in the private security agencies, petrol-pump attendants, domestics, fast-food assistants, hospital auxiliaries and porters come increasingly from Colombia, Chile, Turkey, Sudan, Sri Lanka, Eritrea or Iran. Unlike earlier settler immigrants, these new asylum seekers have no rights of settlement, rarely the right to work, no right to housing or to medical care, and are under constant threat of deportation.

The new black labour force is thus excluded from the traditional protection afforded by unionisation and direct, full-time employment. It is much more likely to be excluded from the housing market: it is estimated that black people, who constitute 5 per cent of the total population, account for at least 60 per cent of London's homeless. They have been marginalised by new forms of immigration control which semi-criminalise their community – virginity testing, rules making it more difficult for grandparents and children of single parents to join their families here, rules to test the validity of marriage and then the intention of marriage, fining airline and shipping companies for bringing passengers to Britain without proper travel documents, using a Channel ferry as a floating detention centre and so on. Within Britain, black people are 10 times more likely to be stopped by the police, more likely if stopped to be cautioned, if cautioned prosecuted and if prosecuted remanded in custody (twice as many remanded blacks are found not guilty as whites). And if imprisoned, research has shown that the black 14 per cent of the prison population are subject to systematic discrimination in the allocation of work.

The cultural position of blacks in Britain has also been under increasing attack. Opting out of local educational control, ostensibly to implement parental choice, opens the way to a segregated system, as demanded by the Dewsbury parents in 1988. Opted-out schools circumvent the Race Relations Act, while the core curriculum significantly does not reflect the multicultural nature of British society. Major cultural events like the Notting Hill Carnival are treated less as a celebration of entertainment than as a problem of public order. And as the general divisions between rich and poor, suburb and inner city, core and periphery have steadily grown throughout the 1980s, blacks in particular have been the victims.

It is surely clear by now that liberal notions of equality of opportunity have had little effect on racial discrimination because the starting line is so manifestly unequal. In practice it implies equal access to differential amounts of power, status, material wealth, whereas the notion of equality entails abolition of these differentials. What is needed now is not mere passive notions of non-discrimination, but positive action programmes with specific goals and timetables attached. This does not mean a rigid quota system without regard to merit or suitability.

Goals and targets to promote minority employment should be the heart of the programme. Goals do not however require the selection of unqualified persons; rather, failure to meet a goal calls for inquiry into the reasons for failure, whereas failure to meet a quota calls for penalties. On this basis, in areas of significant under-representation of blacks in skilled-manual or white-collar jobs, positive action programmes would set target levels for ethnic minority employment, to be achieved within given timescales. Training and recruitment policies would be geared specifically to attain these targets. As a powerful incentive or sanction, success in implementing these programmes should be formally promoted as a principal criterion by which management performance, and therefore pay, is determined.

But it remains critical that the struggle to empower black people is not, and is not seen to be, a process of reverse discrimination. Socialism has never been about promoting the interests of one particular class or group at the expense of others. That is why racial quotas should be repudiated. They derogate from the human dignity and individuality of all to whom they are applied, and they are invidious in principle and practice towards those excluded. Why should blacks be a protected group set apart for special treatment, and not Irish, Slavs or Turks? Quotas can be tokenism of the worst kind, and can actually enhance racism.

The ideal of 'equality of opportunity accompanied by cultural diversity in an atmosphere of mutual tolerance' will not be achieved without new liberating measures. These should include amending the Race Relations Act to reverse the burden of proof, and facilitating 'class actions' (as advocated in Chapter 8). But the key new enforceable measure is positive-action programmes (similar to affirmative action in the US, though some see it as problematic), applied as appropriate in each different context of discrimination, with back-up programmes designed to meet targets and timescales, and constantly monitored to check progress and analyse and remedy shortcomings. Such a plan, systematically pursued to put power in real specific forms into the hands of black people, would for the first time bring them fully into the mainstream of economic and social life.

In summary, the official approach towards poverty, disadvantage and discrimination has traditionally been piecemeal and palliative. It has been designed to ease the experience of humiliation, never to enable the victims to escape it or overcome it. This is because the root cause of all these conditions is powerlessness, and the premise for all official policies of amelioration has always been that the power structure within society should remain intact. Only if that premise is breached by new programmes, such as those outlined here, which consciously seek to alter that power structure by putting real new leverage into the hands of the disadvantaged, will they ever gain the independence to control their own lives.

10
Power-sharing for Efficiency in the Workplace

The 1980s was a decade of momentous economic change. In the West, privatisation and the reassertion of the market were matched, in the East, by the overturning of totalitarian communism and the collapse of command systems like the USSR's Gosplan. Socialism (which is certainly not what existed previously in the Eastern bloc) has been forced to restructure its forms fundamentally, if not its underlying ideas.

Industrial Structure Transformed

On both sides of Europe the market is predominating over central planning because mass production of the 1960s has given way to the flexible specialisation of production in the 1980s, and only a decentralised economy can cope with that change. Mass production in heavy-engineering plants may be appropriate in the early stages of industrialisation, but it will not be the dominant mode at later stages of capitalist development, particularly in the information society spawned by the semi-conductor revolution.

Flexibility, born of the spread of micro-chip technology into every area of production and services, has also begun to transform industrial relations. As key economic variables like inflation levels, exchange rates and energy costs change rapidly and become increasingly unpredictable, the response to uncertainty is sought in speed, flexibility and innovativeness. The tools for this time-based competition aimed at customised delivery are partly IT (computer-aided design, highly adaptive manufacturing systems and electronic data interchange in distribution), but also close employee involvement and a shift from adversarial to partner-like relations with unions and suppliers alike.

As competing in time, market fragmentation, computer link-up from end-user through to supplier, and attention to fast-paced innovation and quality move to the top of the agenda, hierarchy is ceasing to work. Equally, the old-style giants are giving way to smaller-scale inter-linked co-operative networks. Rather than technology, it is the line worker committed to constant improvements and rapidly retrained who is becoming the chief agent for adding value and achieving continuous innovation. Already the typical worker in the new high-tech business or many service businesses is highly trained and has been found to function best in small consultative groups (in British variants of Japanese quality circles), so industrial management is moving socialism's way.

Socialists have no interest in repudiating this new emerging economy simply because it is market-run. Their interest is rather that the decisions as to what is done and how in that market economy, and the resulting rewards, are not overwhelmingly dominated by a small privileged power elite, but much more widely disseminated. In fact, socialists make two claims as to why they can run a decentralised economy (which is not the same as capitalism) *better* than their ideological opponents.

One is that they would improve performance by regulating against the excesses of the market. Market deficiencies like the disregard of external diseconomies, excessive fluctuations in the trade cycle and the financial markets, anti-competitive dominance of the largest companies, and excessive widening of the wealth–poverty gap would all be countered by a judicious mix of tax, regulation and incentives (environmental as well as social). But socialists would also assert, secondly and more importantly, that they, uniquely, can improve performance by opening up opportunities and unlocking energies hitherto suppressed by capitalist society. That is by extending power and incentives, social as well as financial, as well as developing social markets, throughout the economic structure. Power-sharing becomes the partner of efficiency.

Involving Employees to the Full

It is crucial that power-sharing in industrial relations be seen as an opportunity, not a threat. It is not intended to prevent managers talking direct to their workforce, but to encourage it. It is not intended to force any particular structure of employee participation on the workforce. Good communications and shared decision-making should develop organically as far as possible. There is a strong case for giving companies one to two years to implement these proposals or an equivalent variant in their own way before the statutory requirement takes effect. Certainly it should be done slowly, building on experience, not just passing one act like a fire-and-forget missile. Labour should take a leaf out of the Tories' book, who produced six anti-trade union acts and eight anti-social security Acts in a decade.

What is needed is an *enabling* Employee Participation Act which allows employee representatives to choose whichever option they prefer and to trigger it into effect through a ballot. It may mean requiring employers to respond to an extension of the range of collective bargaining so that they begin to negotiate about specific matters that are often at present decided simply by managerial prerogative. Or in the 60 per cent of the economy which is not unionised, it may mean a legal right to set up an independent forum, where at least a minimum agenda of workplace issues are regularly and systematically discussed. Or workplace democracy may develop through technical, financial and managerial assistance in setting up, or converting to, industrial co-operatives. Or it could mean the right of workers to appoint their own worker-directors.

But whatever the form of workplace democracy chosen, the underlying principles are clear. First, the books must be opened and full information on the working of the company must be regularly provided, subject only to the protection of genuine commercial confidentiality (which must not be allowed to be hijacked by management for a blanket cover-up of anything inconvenient).

Second, whatever option is selected, there must be effective access for worker representatives to the point at which decisions are actually made. That may well in the first instance involve issues like health and safety, training, working environment, flexible hours packages and child care arrangements. But steadily over time it should extend to decisions like guidelines on new technology, major training initiatives (or the lack of them), plant closures, major redundancies and takeovers. It is a significant precedent that in Germany an employer cannot sack an individual employee without the agreement of the worker representatives on the works council.

Third, worker representatives must be well-trained and well-resourced. For their role should be not only to assess management proposals, but to contribute cogent and feasible proposals of their own. And they must have the power to ensure they are taken seriously by management. Notoriously the absence of that power led to the sidelining of workers' plans for the revamping of Lucas Aerospace in 1976 when there was a major downturn in defence orders.

Fourth, there must be clear and detailed procedures for settling disagreements within companies. In rare cases where this cannot be achieved, there may be a place for an extended role for the Advisory, Conciliation and Arbitration Service. However, since ACAS operates exclusively by persuasion rather than enforcement, the role should perhaps be filled by regional labour-market bodies. In Germany and Sweden they are highly regarded in providing expertise to help resolve issues like training plans, proposed alternatives to redundancies, and job design.

For both sides of industry these proposals present a challenge and a need to change. Managers will fear it ends their 'right to manage'. But there never was any such right in the first place: management is a skill, not a right. It does mean that managers will lead, not by dint of structural authority, but through the exercise of professional skills. For the unions, it means abandonment of a negative role, passively acquiescent for most of the time, and then kicking management when the workforce erupts. It requires instead a much closer (though not compromised) partnership in the running of companies, with well-trained and experienced workforce representatives deploying a high level of advisory and advocacy skills on a wide range of issues important to their members.

The potential economic benefits are considerable. There is plenty of evidence that innovation in products and processes is carried through more efficiently the greater the involvement of workers and the greater their degree of job discretion. It is also well-established from German experience that requiring companies to justify redundancies to employee representatives biases them away from sackings towards long-term preservation of market share through product innovation and skill upgrading. There is evidence too that getting the planned growth of incomes accepted is easier in economies where workers have greater job security, genuine involvement in decision-making and benefit from training and re-training.

Managing the Managers

British managers are too often under-qualified and under-trained for their crucial role. It reflects partly the British culture which under-values industry and personal competence; partly our confused and class-ridden educational system; and partly under-resourced training in both the public and private sectors. Managers are also largely middle-class in origin, reflecting the class view of social and occupational dominance.

Less than a fifth of managers in Britain have received more than a week's training. Because proper management qualifications are so sparse, a huge number of senior managers in Britain have a background in accountancy – no less than 120,000 in the UK compared with only 4,000 in West Germany and 6,000 in Japan. This may well have contributed to British managers' timidity in investment and enterprise, their emphasis on cost as opposed to value, and the balance-sheet mentality versus human-resource management which has been so much part of Britian's industrial decline. Industry has been consistently under-valued in Britain, and the key role of management has been regularly under-valued by Labour in particular. It is too often seen, wrongly, as being about the mechanistic maximization of profit or output. Conducted at its best, it is a skill aimed at optimum development of the relationships between individuals and organisations, the legitimacy of authority, accountability, and sensitivity to the environment beyond the organisation's direct concern.

Above all, management is a skill which should be opened up to *all* sections of society and not monopolised by traditionally dominant groups. There are thousands of men and women who have substantial latent capacities for people management, but whose talents are wasted because recruitment is rarely sought from the working class. They remain as shop stewards, trade union branch secretaries, convenors, foremen – important posts, but unduly restricting the inspirational skills that many possess.

Access to management must be greatly widened. Career development needs to be opened up within companies so that manual, clerical, technical and administrative grades are not self-contained barriers to advancement, but bases from which service in-training provides a ladder right through to the top. Every manager who has had negligible formal education in the past should be guaranteed the opportunity to study up to at least the Certificate in Business Administration level, at fee costs that are personally affordable by the typical junior manager. And the number of both part-time and full-time student places in management education within universities, polytechnics and colleges must be very substantially increased. A doubling of business undergraduates would still yield less than 10 per cent of national graduate output in Britain, while in the US a quarter of higher education has a majority management component. All this should open up management to a much wider social spectrum.

Equally important is inculcating a new ethos and style of management. It is not about exclusive preoccupation with short-term profit, though longer-term financial objectives do have to be met. It is not about a right to manage (which as such does not exist), but a duty to galvanise. Leadership must be earned; it cannot be imposed. A socialist ethos of management should instil a culture of high standards of service, integrity and commitment to customers, suppliers, employees and shareholders, and enlightened support for high-quality training, equal opportunity, and environmental and community concern.

Three new mechanisms are needed to achieve this. First, a new office of audit of management (similar to the National Audit Office monitoring local government) should be set up, building on strategic management consultancy which is slowly developing in the UK. Its role would be to advise and monitor companies not only in the achievement of traditional objectives like greater efficiency, but also on these wider goals of inter-personal management. For those organisations with the best performance to this end, a new Queen's Award for Management would be granted. Second, tax incentives should be used to entrench pay systems that reward managers in accordance with these criteria. And third, a group of new public sector training colleges should be established to inculcate these values in persons training for management jobs in the public service.

But what if managers turn out to be incompetent, lazy, mediocre or simply not up to the job? Removing them should not have to depend on the sack from superiors, who may be incompetent too. Nor can reliance be placed on market forces. Shareholders are too fragmented, largely ignorant of the day-to-day condition of the firm and usually uninterested, and almost always unorganised. Institutional shareholders rarely intervene except in extreme cases. And to rely on market collapse as the ultimate check on managerial incompetence is to pull down perhaps hundreds of other employees through no fault of their own.

One solution would be for a works council (or some other elected committee of employee representatives), if they were seriously dissatisfied with a particular manager, to pass a vote of no confidence in him, with the reasons clearly spelt out. That resolution plus the reasons would then be passed to the Board or the relevant senior management level responsible, and if they ratified it, he would be moved or dismissed. If not, the grievances would be discussed between the two sides and a period of some six months allowed to rectify them. If they were not and the employees passed a further vote of no confidence, the matter would be referred to the arbitration of the regional labour market board whose decision, after full investigation, would be binding.

Developing Social Markets

Other ways too are needed to open up industrial opportunity for those whom lack of capital rendered powerless in the past. A precedent exists from the Thatcherite agenda in the 1980s. One of its important characteristics was the careful selection of new agents on the ground put in place to carry through the change in culture desired. This involved not only the stimulation of many more small-scale capitalists through venture capital and the enterprise allowance scheme, but more significant examples like Urban Development Corporations to supersede elected local authorities, the London Docks Development Corporation to mastermind one of the biggest industrial redevelopment schemes in Europe, Housing Action Trusts to deal with inner city decay, and district general managers to inculcate commercialisation into the NHS.

Thatcher's model was always built round private capital as the source of power. Socialism needs *its own* alternative model of development. In particular, socialism for its part needs vigorously to generate *its own* 'social entrepreneurs', that is, those using their entrepreneurial skills to achieve public social ends rather than private commercial ends. There are several means to promote this, all of which should be pursued.

Encouraging Social Entrepreneurs Without Capital

Stimulating communities and workforces to draw up lists of facilities and skills that they possess has a dramatic effect in raising local consciousness. The Greater London Enterprise Board (GLEB) pioneered this approach by building up a product bank of socially useful products and services already related to known needs, and then making it available to co-operatives and other enterprises looking for new products to maintain or expand employment. By building prototypes or short-batch production of such products or services, they developed a form of technological agitprop to raise awareness about the potential of 'social markets'.

On this basis a system of regional and local 'hearings' should be held throughout the country, involving consultations with trade unions, community organisations and other representative local bodies, in order to begin a preliminary assessment of the scale of outstanding unmet needs. From this at least a rough estimate could be prepared of the kind of unused labour and productive resources which would be available to meet those needs. The GLC and GLEB experience, both in London Dockland and the now devastated industrial headland of west London, shows that working people offer an immensely rich repository of creative ideas.

The need for 'social innovators' is manifest. Are we as a people so well housed, so well served with hospitals, schools, transport networks and basic social infrastructure that there is nothing constructive for half a million unemployed building workers to do? Is access to kidney dialysis and other specialist medical equipment now so ready for the chronic sick that there is no useful work for under-employed scientists, technologists and engineers? Are the elderly so well-heated and free of risk from hypothermia that there is no work for those with skills to adapt energy-saving devices and to construct cheaper, more accessible heating systems? Why are workers who design and build water storage, pumping and treatment equipment, redundant when millions in Third-World countries die every year of water-borne illnesses and bad sanitation?

There are several reasons why at present such urgent social need is left unmet. The recipients in need do not command the necessary resources – there is a deficiency of effective demand. Unemployment is deliberately used in a capitalist system as a regulator to reduce overheating in the economy. Public expenditure is constrained by the alleged disincentive effect of higher taxation. All of these objections need to be specifically addressed (and are, respectively in Chapters 5, 12 and pp 128–31 of this chapter).

Another rationale for encouraging social, not just commercial, entrepreneurs lies in overriding strict economic viability by the concepts of social opportunity and social cost. The difference between production for market profit and for social need is not as stark as is often supposed. The margin of economic resources required to make an 'unviable' project 'viable' is often just that, 'marginal'. The practicality of this is shown by the fact that GLEB created several thousand jobs in the mid-1980s at an average cost of a little over £4,000 each, when the cost to the community of keeping a worker with a wife and two children unemployed for a year came to (combining benefit costs with tax foregone) over £5,000, let alone the cost of up to £70,000 per job in 'free market' schemes such as enterprise zones.

Balancing Social Against Commercial Objectives

Another means to develop social markets, and the widened opportunities and increased employment that go with them, lies in the generation of 'social incentives'. These may take two forms. The stronger version involves the cultivation of moral or altruistic incentives, that is, those prompted by a vicarious concern for the benefit of others or the wider community rather than the self-gain of financial incentives.

One valuable means of inculcating concern for others as a basis for citizenship would be a re-structuring of tertiary education and training to include a six or twelve-month period of community service. This might involve, unpaid at trainee rates of support, working in local community projects and services, environmental landscaping, hospital care services, participation on building or maintenance projects, or similar experience designed to widen understanding of community life and develop non-self-interested motives. But such an innovation would only have positive effect if it was embedded in a prior educational curriculum that emphasised socialist values such as sharing, community co-op-eration and altruism.

The weaker version of social incentives involves the use of financial rewards to advance social goals. Such corporate social goals should include power-sharing (extending the area of joint decision-making within their own organisations), equal employ-ment opportunities (for blacks and disabled people), equal rights for part-time workers, change where necessary to environment-friendly products and processes, and an 'ethical dimension' in investments. All of these would extend power and open up new opportunities for disadvantaged groups. The inducements used to ensure these objectives are carried through would vary according to what was most appropriate, from 'soft' incentives (grants and tax reliefs) to more formal ones (legislative require-ments or contract compliance).

There are several instruments through which this transfer of power can be secured. One, which is in its infancy, is the spread of local enterprise boards. Three in particular have already scored notable successes even in the face of an inhospitable economic environment – Greater London (before it was dismantled at the abolition of the GLC), West Midlands and Lancashire Enterprise Boards. GLEB's record offers clear lessons. It operated either through taking total ownership (especially in companies bought from the receiver), an equity stake usually above 25 per cent, and/or loans. But experience showed that neither a formal ownership share for the workforce nor their representation by some worker directors were as effective in gaining control over major decisions as strong trade union organisation. GLEB therefore concentrated on achieving unionisation and procedural agreements as the basis for extending democratic structures through their companies. In some this was effected through establishing a new 'plenary committee' which met quarterly and was attended by the convenor, the chair of the shop stewards' committee, the trade union official, the managing director, the manufacturing director and the GLEB chair of the board.

Several key problems emerged. One was the obvious conflict between commercial and social objectives. The GLC required GLEB investments to become profitable after two years, which meant that equal employment opportunities – for training, wage changes, adaptations to buildings for disabled people, nursery provision and so on – sometimes had to be temporarily shelved where market survival was at stake. Clearly social incentives cannot override commercial necessity, but they should supplement it wherever feasible. Another problem has been that GLC officials, inherited from the previous regime, were sometimes obstructive towards the deployment of social goal pressures. If social markets are to work, key players must be ideologically committed and sympathetic ('red experts' as they have been called).

Third, worker directors are of no use in the face of hostile management and weak trade union organisation. A clear lesson of widespread GLEB experience has been the need to provide training in specialist management skills on a large scale. And fourth, social objectives need to be embodied in separate 'social plans' so that funding decisions can be based explicitly on precise measurement of whether or not they have been achieved.

A New Role for the Public Sector

The public sector also has a major role to play in power transfer. The reasons why public ownership was established in the first place are now re-emerging – abuse of monopoly power (British Gas as an unregulated private monopoly), neglect of investment and R&D (the water utilities while awaiting privatisation neglect pollution control and sewer collapses), low-quality standards (privatised cleaning breaks performance contracts), profit-creaming in neglect of public interest (privatised buses cut routes and force up fares while transport de-regulation generates congestion), failure to re-structure (lack of co-operation between military technological innovation and civilian diffusion, or between branch plants in the wider economy) and so on. But a very important additional objective can be achieved through a selective public sector revival.

That is to extend choice and power. That does not mean Tory choice which, as illustrated by the de-regulation of buses, school vouchers, the licensing of Mercury telephones, and private health, involves skimming off the best without regard to the losers. By contrast, socialist choice means a wider choice which protects rights and opportunities for *all*, not just the minority with money to buy their way out.

The significance of public ownership is not that ownership necessarily implies power or that power requires ownership. It is rather that without power over the controlling key to the system, it is almost impossible to overcome hostile managers. In that context it is crucial to note – what some sections of the left still seem resolutely unable to see – that changes in the structure of capitalism over the last decade or two mean that control of factory production is often no longer the key. The key lies rather in many cases in control of the new technology and control of fast-changing distribution and marketing systems. New techniques are constantly evolving, with more sub-contracting and franchising, and increasingly flexible systems that allow short runs and rapid adjustment according to demand. Indeed the development in manufacturing of integrated Euro-wide or global operations means that nationalisation old-style leaves government in control of the valleys, not the commanding heights. Moreover it is clearly unsuited as a response to the burgeoning service sector of the economy, which in the US now embraces three-fifths of all economic activity.

The public sector should maximise the power it already has. The spin-off from military R&D should be used positively to promote civilian applications of technology, especially for small and specialist firms searching out a niche in the market. Government should not tie its hands behind its back by blunting its power over tariffs and the exchanges in its dealings with multi-nationals through the principle of non-discrimination; subject to GATT obligations, it should use their levels as bargaining counters with individual firms. Instead of allowing private capital to use its mobile guerilla units against the baroque batallions of the public sector, government should use its resources to maximise new techniques. One way would be to set up a substantial grant fund from which innovations both inside the public sector and in the voluntary/co-operative sector could be funded, with breakthroughs then being generalised throughout the industry or service.

In addition, public purchasing has an enormous reach since central government final consumption of goods and services amounted to no less than £92 billion in 1988. Of course public purchasing is rightly aimed to get the best value for money, and where a significant margin of gain lies with one particular buy over others, clearly that should override other external factors. But where bids in terms of value for money are fairly equal, government should make clear that they will vigorously operate a preference system in favour of companies that meet prescribed social objectives.

Another mechanism lies in the panoply of reliefs and grants offered by government to channel corporate development in particular directions. In 1989–90 British industry was awarded income tax relief, corporation tax allowances, double tax relief, and a reduced rate of corporation tax on small and medium-sized companies which amounted in total to £11.5 billion. In addition, general industrial and regional support, scientific and technological assistance to industry, and selective industrial aid added a further £2 billion to industry's coffers. Government should make clear that this range of reliefs and grants, and in particular the corporation tax capital allowances worth £8.5 billion, are awarded in full only to those companies satisfying a social audit. Such an audit would spell out environmental objectives, fair employment practices, information disclosure and industrial democracy targets.

A whole variety of new strategems should be developed to entrench within the heart of the economy the essential public sector role of extending power and opportunities now suppressed by the private market. Community enterprise should be encouraged with a distinctively public sector ethos of benefiting those currently excluded by market pricing. Thus councils should be prompted to set up 'property shops' to compete with estate agents and promote community-based construction agencies which would tender for large-scale house-building purchasable at reasonable prices. And municipalities should be encouraged to issue bonds to promote local employment, with holders of these public bonds being awarded special preferential bonuses (for example free phone calls on Sunday for BT bond holders over 65).

Co-operatives and the Market

Another means to extend power and opportunity in a decentralised economy is to introduce the right to convert a privately owned company into an industrial co-operative. The conventional view on the left has been that markets are exploitative, profits are bad, planning is good and nationalisation is the real objective. But if what is wrong with markets is that they give much more power to some than to others, the remedy is not nationalisation, but equalising that power in the market-place. That is the justification for co-operative enterprises where control is vested in the workers and the non-voting equity spread equally among all workers.

Co-operatives (unlike employee share ownership schemes or ESOPS) *do* represent a real sharing of power , but there are lessons to be learnt in their development. One is that rescuing ailing private sector firms on the point of liquidation and transforming them into co-operatives – like the Benn co-operatives in 1974–5 at Meriden, IPC, and Scottish Daily News – is almost certain to fail because their economic viability is by then already too damaged. They should be launched as on-going enterprises in a well-tested market.

Another problem is that producer co-operatives tend to react more slowly to changes in market conditions which capitalist firms on the other hand are more likely to see as creating profitable opportunities to be quickly exploited. The moral is surely that if in good times co-operative firms are too sluggish to remain at the sharp end of high-demand or high technology markets, they should steer clear of areas with variable demand, harsh competition and rapid technical advance.

Another issue concerns investment. Where co-operatives are unhappy about accepting 'excessive' external financing because of loss of control, they are clearly unsuited to production which requires capital-intensive techniques. This suggests that the co-operative form is more likely to succeed in areas of relatively small-scale production which rely disproportionately on the skills of the entire labour force (rather than on the capital or the talents of a small group) and in relatively well-established markets and product lines.

Capital and tax incentives are needed to encourage both the establishment of new co-operatives from scratch and the conversion of existing enterprises. For the latter purpose, government should offer tax compensation for sellers whose whole enterprises are sold to their workforces at below market prices. This could make worker buy-outs a favoured solution for many family businesses facing a succession problem as well as by conglomerates seeking to divest themselves of some peripheral activity. Equally, where any public sector function is sold off (for example garbage collection or British Rail catering), government should treat co-operatives or workforce companies of ex-employees as preferential buyers or tenderers. If in addition government were to make a revamped co-operative development agency into a major resource for financial, technical and managerial expertise for new or converting co-operative enterprises, this sector could within a decade be playing a major role in the fast-growing small business goods and service sector.

There are further variants of this model which should be tested and applied. One is capital–labour partnerships which hold out a way of combining the benefits of self-management with some of the economic advantages of the orthodox capitalist firm. These are run with an agreed division of rights and responsibilities between the two sides, and a corresponding division of profits. Unlike conventional co-operatives, partnerships of this kind will be more inclined to expand employment in the face of market opportunities, since employment levels will be decided by the holders of capital. They would also be more appropriate in highly uncertain markets where the members of an orthodox co-operative would be unwilling to bear the full quota of risk.

This does of course reintroduce potential conflict between one party whose interests are solely in levels of profit and the other whose interests are more diverse – not only profit levels, but flexible and varied work, length of working day, and so on. Yet self-management will only survive, and only be worthwhile, if workers have not only an economic stake in their enterprise but play an active part in the real decision-making.

This is one answer to the insider–outsider problem of co-operatives whereby in a situation of market expansion the established worker has a preference for more pay over the unemployed outsider's preference for more jobs even at existing pay. Another solution is offered by the 'revenue-sharing' economy popularised by Martin Weitzman of MIT. He notes that if, for example, a worker is paid a straight wage of £100, he will be taken on only if he adds at least £100 to value added, but if instead he is paid an £80 wage plus £20 as a share of overall profits, he will be employed as long as his marginal contribution exceeds £80. Thus so long as government and central banks maintain the growth of *nominal* demand, more jobs will be provided and inflation reduced – an exceptionally important economic objective in any case. But the snag is that as more workers are taken on, revenue per head – and thus the existing workers' profit share – will decline because of the need to reduce prices or promote the sale of more output.

The solution should be a *discriminating* labour–capital partnership under which workers are part-owners and participate in decisions without undermining new recruitment. But the price of this might have to be that successful firms would initially offer new entrants fewer labour shares – that is, lower wages – than established employees. That might be the condition for satisfying both insiders and outsiders in a part-co-operativised economy. But in a Thatcherite framework of de-regulation and privatisation there has been resistance (not very effective) to contracting more work to outside suppliers with lower pay scales or to franchising at different pay rates.

What all these proposals emphasise is that a feasible socialist market economy would be pluralistic. There would be a large co-operative sector, a sector in which capital–labour partnerships were formed in varying proportions around a 50:50 norm, a sector of worker buy-outs of larger firms (like the National Freight Corporation where the share price was set to safeguard the controlling interest of the employees), as well as a sector taking a conventional capitalist form. In addition, basic industries requiring massive levels of investment – such as oil, coal, electricity, telecommunications – would be state-managed or at least very closely state-regulated, even though subject to (mainly international) market competition. But the key thread underlying this pluralistic structure would be the across-the-board redistribution of power within the market away from the traditional elite of capital-holders to the broader workforce.

Access to Databases as a New Source of Power

In the information society, power over services can be secured in other non-market ways too. A national broad-band fibre optic cable network should be installed throughout the country to act as a new information highway into every living room, classroom and workplace. Broad-band cable can carry all the services currently delivered by telephone wires, radio, TV and satellite broadcast, but its great merit is that it is two-way. It will be the new electronic highway, not only providing new choices for consumers, but offering new patterns for work with huge implications for corporate structures.

Broad-band cable will, for example, allow such consumer exotics as individual dialling to video libraries for individually transmitted films or training programmes. It will permit home-based shopping, immediate information not only on transport timetables but on whether a particular bus or train is running to time, and improved home security. On one dimension it is a democratic technology that potentially can enormously extend the consumer's power to choose in a multitude of new ways.

However, its employment implications are likely to be far more far-reaching. The capacity of domestic computer databases to plug into national information networks opens up the perspective of groupings of informal, self-motivating work units that are flexible, information-based, and consumer-directed. The work environment of the early twenty-first century will be based on the networking of community activists and interest-group lobbyists. It will radically alter employment patterns and herald the end of commuting: work is transmitted to the employee rather than employees being centralised around work.

The significance of networking goes further still. It represents the disintegration of corporate and bureaucratic power in the face of downstream participation in the economy and politics. Strong hierarchies like Ford Motors may simply be too slow to adapt. Political power, like commercial profit, will lie in applying creative minds to flows of knowledge, not in charismatic leaders and managers ordering disciplined masses of workers.

The information revolution thus opens up a fundamental divide. The market approach would lead to a haphazard combination of cabling in wealthy areas and satellite television more generally, which would inhibit individual responsiveness among the nation at large to what was received. A radical non-market approach based on the interactive information network stimulated by democratic cabling could, on the other hand, achieve that diffusion of wealth and power which has always been the heart of the socialist vision. But the implications of the new technology run deep. By enabling services currently provided by public sector agencies to be provided in a more individual and effective (and also non-market) way, it exposes the left institutions of Fordism – the Morrisonian public corporation, the district general hospital, the comprehensive school, the tower block or even the large trade union – as the anachronisms they are steadily becoming.

11

Making Finance Work
for the People

The unfolding Maxwell saga in 1992 has brought home to many, more starkly than ever before, the sheer greed and selfishness of so much financial wheeling and dealing. But the City under our system of finance capitalism has never worked in the interests of the broad mass of the population, except incidentally. Democratising the power of the City is probably the single most important task of a radical reforming government because the City has always traditionally overridden the interests of Britain as a whole, and of British industry in particular, in pursuit of the very short-term interests of its financial institutions. The means to democratise that power should follow the central theme of this book: power-sharing wherever possible, regulation where strictly necessary. Both must be deployed in the City.

It is profoundly anti-democratic that, with just over 30 funds accounting for almost two-thirds of pension-fund assets of over a quarter of a trillion pounds, some 50 fund-investment managers are in control of the new commanding heights – the disposition of enormous sums of capital accumulated from the required savings of millions of workers. Merchant banks such as Hill Samuel, Schroder Wagg, Morgan Grenfell, and Warburg, together with stockbrokers like Phillips and Drew, manage these huge sums according to their own investment policy, with only the most vague and general guidance from the funds' trustees. One result has been that the bank investment managers have invested more and more heavily in the shares of the *same* financial sector, mainly clearing banks and insurance companies, that manage these funds. This self-serving and self-perpetuating set-up needs to be opened to the winds of democratic change.

A New System of Corporate Governance

Institutional investors have great power over the economy and very little responsibility either to the companies they effectively control or to the public. They were mainly the cause of the takeover and buy-out mania of the 1980s, with its legacy of over-leveraged companies, defaulted junk bonds, and short-sighted management policies. A stock exchange system where institutional investors hold two-thirds of the equity of the whole of British industry lends itself to abuse by corporate raiders whose only objective is their own enrichment. Significantly our trading rivals in Japan and Germany are virtually free of hostile takeovers, and it is no accident that their systems encourage long-term planning and investment.

What is needed is a new system of corporate sovereignty – one that removes the pressure on directors to maximise share prices in the short run and the pressure on institutional investors to sell out good, successful, well-managed companies whenever someone offers a premium on the market price. That points to a quinquennial cycle instead of the usual annual meeting for shareholders, with directors being elected for five-year terms. They would stand for election on the company's record over the last five years and its strategic plan for the next five years. The election statement would contain details of industry and stock market averages providing past comparisons, together with the assumptions on which the company's projections over the next five years are based.

These elections would often be contested. It should be established that a proportion of the votes, perhaps a third, should be allocated ex officio to the workforce for the purpose of these elections. It should also be laid down that any group of shareholders with at least 5 per cent of the outstanding shares or with shares having an aggregate market value of at least £5 million, or any group within the workforce comprising at least a third of the total, would have the same access to the corporate proxy machinery as the management.

If shareholders and employees decided to contest the quinquennial election, they could do so on the basis that if elected they would offer the company for sale. Alternatively, they could give their support for a bid made by a third party. Either way, the system would put maximum pressure on directors to succeed in their prime role of choosing competent managers and holding them to achieve their business plans. But it would also eliminate hostile takeovers between the five-year intervals. Instead it would facilitate negotiated acquisitions, especially equity mergers that avoid high leverage and would not over-burden the combined companies with debt. Above all, the five-yearly system, by preventing hostile takeovers, would permit companies to pursue long-term planning (as they do in Germany and Japan) without fear that investment in R&D, plant and equipment, efforts to extend market share and similar short-term depressants on earnings might result in a takeover.

Such a system would provide stability, but not immobility. If within the five-year cycle a company failed to achieve, say, 80 per cent of its projections for two consecutive years, the rules could empower holders of 20 per cent of the shares and/or half the workforce to call a special interim meeting to which all the requirements of the quinquennial meeting would apply. In addition, mediocre or incompetent management – so often typified by high top salaries, share options confined to a handful of apparatchiks, and generous golden parachutes – would be subject to permanent pressure from *below*, through the procedures for their removal outlined in Chapter 5.

But most of all, this new framework of corporate control would for the first time put power into the hands of the workforce to play a major and maybe decisive role in determining their own future and that of their company. Gone would be the days when the fate of their own company was traded above their heads without even a gesture of consultation and their jobs and careers staked out at the mercy of forces over which they had not an iota of control. It would correctly establish corporate governance as ultimately the shared responsibility of both the shareholders and the workforce, not the prerogative to be monopolised by either one or the other. It would end the malign influence of transitory professional investors, risk arbitrageurs, junk bonds and insider dealing corporate raiders who are solely self-seeking. It is a classic example of how putting power into the hands of ordinary people most affected is not only right and just, but can achieve a fundamental improvement in economic performance.

Re-regulation of Financial Markets

But it is not only a matter of making institutional investors share power with employees and commit themselves more closely to the companies they partly control. There is also an overwhelming need to change the locus of control in pension funds themselves. De-regulation of financial markets has enthroned international financial institutions in the dominant role in contemporary capitalism. Making these enormous concentrations of financial power reflect the needs of the broad majority of the population, rather than force local and national economies to conform to the priorities of financial markets, requires a dual thrust of reform.

National Financial Markets

Partly it requires regulation: new social criteria to govern takeovers; re-regulation of financial markets, especially regarding the creation of credit; new rules determining investment priorities for pension and insurance funds; tighter supervision of City activities to control or minimise stock-market scandals; and new banking policies aimed at producing more stable market conditions and cheaper credit for approved purposes. But most of all it requires setting in place new mechanisms for people at large, or their elected representatives, to have access to this financial power and to direct it in the public interest of the wider population.

The most important and immediate regulatory requirement is re-regulation of the financial markets. The abolition of exchange controls in October 1979, followed by the removal of the 'corset' on bank lending (that is, the supplementary special deposits scheme which penalised banks that expanded their lending by more than a permitted rate) in June 1980, paved the way to the uncontrolled and extremely damaging credit boom of the mid-1980s. The ensuing battle between the banks and the building societies in the loans-for-housing market drove lending sky-high: while the annual increase in their lending during 1977–80 had been about 5 per cent of GDP, by 1982 it had risen to a staggering 35 per cent of GDP and to 36 per cent in 1984.

The most significant, and disturbing, aspect of this process was the enormous growth in 'equity withdrawal', where house-buyers borrow more than they strictly need and use the surplus to buy video recorders, cars, yachts or other expensive consumer commodities. Equity withdrawal grew from about £1 billion a year in 1979 to no less than £22 billion at its peak in 1988.

The effect of this phenomenon on monetary policy has been devastating. It has reversed the effect that inflation has on consumers, and made government economic management far harder. Previously inflation, by eroding money savings, encour-aged people on balance to save more. In the 1980s, however, after financial de-regulation, people found it easy to tap the increase in their wealth-in-housing that inflation had caused, so they did not need to save as hard. Because people were obliged to save less, they could spend more. Whereas inflation used to be partly self-correcting (encouraging people to save more and spend less), it gradually became in the 1980s self-reinforcing (encouraging people to save less and spend more). That meant that to hold credit and demand in check, real interest rates had to be kept very much higher than before.

It is clear that a measure of financial re-regulation should have two objectives: to prevent excessive bank lending and to place a bar or disincentive on equity withdrawal. The latter might be achieved through a capital gains tax charge, especially if housing equity withdrawal were lumped together with other forms of taxable gains so that any expansion of debt would draw the CGT net tighter. In addition, moves to make the rights of mortgage lenders over the borrower's property unenforceable in law where the loan exceeds 85 per cent or 95 per cent of the value of the property might usefully reinforce prudent banking practice without necessarily involving high political costs.

The former needs to be addressed by new credit controls on both lenders and borrowers. For lending banks a revised version of the Supplementary Special Deposits Scheme is required, to reduce pressure otherwise falling on interest rates alone and to exert an important psychological effect on bank attitudes. While credit controls following the abolition of exchange controls might not work in wholesale markets, they certainly retain a role in retail markets. Both the German and French authorities use direct controls, including rules governing bank reserves requirements, in a support role for higher interest rates.

Other regulatory requirements include new rules on the investment priorities of pension and insurance funds. Limits should be imposed on the percentage of fund holdings invested in property or overseas (say 5 per cent for the former and 15 per cent for the latter) in order to ensure that a UK manufacturing revival becomes the investment priority. For lack of medium/long-term finance to British industry at comparable cost to its overseas competitors has long been one of its major drawbacks. Indeed Professor Mayer of the City University Business School indicted the City in 1987 for its fundamental failure to allocate capital to its most productive use. Analysing the funding of Britain's capital stock 1970–84 he showed that only 4 per cent of the corporate sector's total funding came from issues of new shares – even though by 1986 brokers were annually charging commissions on equities of some £570 million and the difference between the jobbing system's best buying and selling prices exceeded £1.5 billion. This reveals the very high price currently paid in transaction costs to provide liquidity in a market which in aggregate finances virtually no productive investment.

This huge failure certainly justifies regulation of pension and insurance fund investment. But it is justified by other considerations too. First, the scale of annual income to the funds, in excess of £20 billion, is so enormous that its allocation can closely influence overall national economic performance. Second, market decision-making left to itself has a distinctly unprepossessing record: over the 20-year period to 1985 the average real rate of return of the pension funds was 1 per cent negative. Third, other main European countries exercise similar restraints. In France, insurance companies are subject to an official list of permitted investments, commercial banks can hold only one-fifth of their assets in equities, and loans are allocated by the Credit National in accordance with priorities in the National Plan. In Germany, the insurance sector is closely controlled and cannot invest more than a fifth of its funds in equities. In the US there are severe restrictions on bank lending for property.

It is also necessary to stop the frenetic pace of takeovers, whether the stampede towards the fashion of conglomerate 'synergy' in the 1970s or towards the reverse in the 1980s in the form of Goldsmith-type unbundling, or the short-term financial asset-stripping at the expense of long-term industrial investment exemplified by Hanson. This neglect of long-term industrial commitment would be checked by the new system of corporate governance outlined on pages 137–8. But it should also be more directly addressed by reversing the burden of proof and requiring the predator to demonstrate that the proposed takeover did positively advance the public interest. The relevant criteria would go far beyond the present limit of concern with competition policy and include job creation, industrial expansion and the UK balance of payments.

International Financial Markets

Regulation of the City cannot succeed, however, without regard to the international context of the development of a global capital market. Having established itself as the chief financial centre in the European time zone, the City now provides a service mainly to foreign governments, corporations and financial institutions, not British manufacturers. It takes a percentage cut in the huge capital flows that stem from trade imbalances and financial volatility, thriving rather like a drug company in an epidemic. For it has been a major beneficiary of the collapse of the Bretton Woods fixed-exchange rate system and the widespread removal of exchange controls. In effect, the central bankers' traditional job of stabilising currencies has been privatised. Thus multinationals like ICI or General Motors engage in constant arbitrage through a host of new financial instruments such as swaps to minimise currency and interest-rate risks and to reduce the cost of borrowing.

However, there are already signs that any wider benefits in terms of market efficiency could be outweighed both by the risk of a major shock to the whole system and by intolerable complications for national monetary policy and prudential supervision. The swap market is moving into remoter currencies. Euro-equity paper often carries no voting rights and therefore no influence over management. Eurobonds impose minimal restrictions on the borrower in the form of balance-sheet ratios or levels of interest cover. Above all, major off-balance-sheet risks arise in the case of Euro-notes.

The trend towards 'securitisation', whereby lending is channelled through markets in the form of tradable paper instead of through the banking system, has disturbing implications. If securitised paper fails, as many suspect, to be genuinely marketable when several creditors of a single debtor try to liquidate their holdings at once, a major international breakdown could occur. On these grounds, for example, a savage bear market could kill the Euro-equity market. The Cross Report, published by BIS in 1986, argued that with more credit flowing outside normal banking channels there will not only be less supervision and less complete information, but also a dangerous under-pricing of many of the new financial instruments relative to their inherent risks.

Lending by older people at the top of banks has been replaced by the playing of new markets in securitised paper by a mathematically inclined younger generation busily concocting complex new instruments. Indeed the rate of financial innovation is such that re-regulating markets in an international high-technology environment, though very necessary, will be quite difficult, and even new devices (like the Hattersley proposal to encourage the repatriation of investment funds through the tax system) could be severely diluted.

But the most serious question of all is whether total freedom of capital movements can be reconciled with less free trade in goods and services, in a world of marked payments imbalances – shades of the bankers' ramp followed by economic collapse in the 1920s. For the ability of international debtors (for example many Third World oil producers, now joined ominously by the US) to service their debt is heavily dependent on the maintenance of an open trading system. De-regulation in the early 1980s served both US and UK financial interests, but at the expense of their trading interests because of huge over-valuation of the pound 1980–1 and of the dollar 1983–5.

Another dimension of the same issue is that liberalisation has opened up the prospects for financial crime as never before. Modern communications, a 'loyalty-free' environment ('every man for himself') with market operators switching within and between different firms and centres, immense reservoirs of black money to work with, availability of safe bolt-holes (especially Switzerland, but also dozens of offshore islands), a growing number of accountants and lawyers willing to facilitate the hideaway schemes on a 'no questions asked' basis, non-disclosure of discovered crime to protect market credibility in a PR age, paper-thin Chinese walls, no checks or controls on movement of funds or use of nominee/trustee holdings, and the increasingly casino mentality at large – all these together have altogether overwhelmed current policing, such as it is.

Furthermore, with the removal of the previous stringent controls like pegged exchange rates, credit and interest rate ceilings, tight limits on international capital mobility, strict demarcation lines for financial institutions, and now the rise of endless financial innovation, monetary policy has been undermined utterly. The authorities find it much more complex and difficult to define money, and certainly have little idea how to control a given aggregate. Thus interest rates in Britain in the mid-1980s may have been at the 'wrong' level for several years because of the difficulty of interpreting extraordinarily rapid credit growth. We may well now have reached the point where the cost to the industrial economy of excessively high and volatile real interest rates swamps the putative micro-economic efficiency gains from de-regulating financial markets.

Nor does greater reliance on exchange-rate mechanisms like the EMS offer a compromise solution in a period of monetary uncertainty. For the very factors that have undermined monetary targets have also undermined exchange-rate management. The EMS has been quite tranquil so far largely because it contains only one main currency (the D-mark), because it has been buttressed by capital controls (now being dismantled), and because member countries have been slow to join the financial innovation bandwagon. To that extent the EMS reflects, not a brave new world of de-regulated but orderly financial markets, but a benign throwback to the pre-1971 era of controls.

For all these reasons there is an overwhelming economic and political (not to mention moral and cultural) imperative for bringing the Euro-markets and the explosive growth of securitisation for international financial trading firmly under new prudential supervisory controls. It will require extensive inter-governmental agreement at G7 and EEC levels, but the ideological climate that fostered liberalisation in capital markets has been steadily altering since the Plaza Hotel intervention in exchange markets in 1985 and the recognition of the need for capital controls to support any new system of exchange rate targets developed by G7. It will require central banks to place clear limits on the role of financial innovation by the big US investment houses and UK merchant banks so as to ensure that greater efficiency, in reduced borrowing costs and enhanced liquidity for investors, does not threaten the viability of the whole system or produce off-setting costs to the real economy that far outweigh financial gains in individual deals. It will also require the enforcement, after the collapse of US junk bond dealers Drexel Burnham Lambert in 1989 and the sudden disappearance of apparently strong and growing UK companies like Coloroll in 1990, of a much tougher framework for merger and goodwill accounting, off-balance sheet manipulation and inflation accounting.

Widening Control Over the Pension Funds

A major new framework of prudential supervision for both national and international financial markets is clearly urgently needed to restore balance within the open trading system and to protect the Western economies against the real and growing threat of a major breakdown causing widespread economic dislocation. But a socialist policy requires in addition that the massively over-centralised power locked up within the financial institutions should be opened up to the broad mass of the population who are after all the original collective source of that financial muscle.

The most important new mechanism required concerns control of the pension funds. In 30 years institutional ownership of British companies has risen from a quarter to nearly two-thirds. The largest is the Prudential controlling funds of £34 billion, and the largest 30 altogether control funds estimated at £438 billion in 1990. The wider interests of the pension fund members themselves are rarely taken into account.

A new legal framework for pension fund trustees should be set up which will secure a majority of voting rights for elected representatives of fund members. This would reflect the principle which should be established that each fund's money, being deferred pay, belongs to the members from the day it goes into the fund, not merely from the time that benefits are paid. At present, employers and fund managers claim that the employer is responsible simply for providing the benefits and that until that point the employees have no rights. The Inland Revenue have further complicated the position by ruling that trust deeds had to include the employer as residuary legatee. A new pensions law therefore should settle unmistakably that pension funds belong to their members, including the employer's contributions which are part of the overall employment package for recruiting and retaining suitable employees. Once established as a legal principle, that would then stop the present abuse of pension funds whereby employers cream off any actuarial surplus, and would also fully protect pension funds from being raided as a result of the takeover of the parent company.

Conventional wisdom also has it that trustees are required to invest exclusively where they expect the capital return to be maximised. In fact, within existing law trustees already can put money into what are often called 'social' investments and can look at the interests of members as *employees* as well as pensioners (although that does not necessarily mean investing directly in your own company). In line with this, the new pensions law should unequivocally redefine the trustee duty as being to 'invest responsibly in the interests of the beneficiaries' and according to the objectives of the fund. That would not always mean getting the highest short-term rate of return, as opposed to longer-term economic interests – that would be up to the trustees to decide. Trust deeds should be standardised in accordance with statute, not left to employers' discretion, and would lay down that investment powers should stay with the trustees, not with the firm or any outside body.

Training for the employee representatives will be essential if they are to utilise these new powers fully and not simply defer to the investment managers. Training should therefore be a statutory right for trustees, paid for if necessary out of the fund. Training courses should be laid on by trade unions or professional organisations, and if approved, individuals attending could be eligible for a grant. There should also be a statutory right for a minority of trustees to obtain alternative advice from outside experts, even if the rest of the trustees disagreed or thought it unnecessary.

Capital Funds for Ordinary People

By far the most significant means of extending financial power to the population at large is by exposing decision-making in existing financial institutions to more democratic influences. But over and above that a series of imaginative options can be developed whereby financial opportunity, instead of being locked up as the prerogative of an elite, can be broadened to a much wider range of players in a market economy.

Credit Unions

One option is credit unions which can give assistance on better than market terms to persons on low incomes who may have been excluded from or exploited by mainstream financial institutions. Credit unions are savings and loans co-operatives (a concept regrettably tarnished by S and L 'thrift' collapses in the US in 1989–90) whose members have a common bond of occupation, association or residence. They save with it by investing in the society's shares, and these savings provide a fund out of which low-interest loans are granted to members (at a rate of 1 per cent a month or 12.7 per cent a year, compared with loan sharks money-lending at anything from 60–1,000 per cent). A dividend is also paid to members on their shares out of the surplus that should result from lending at interest.

Essentially they are community banks for low-income groups, but fulfilling this role means prosperous members should be prevented from hijacking the management and activities of the union. They offer a good way of partly relieving the burden of consumer debt, by providing a safe environment for debtors to recover a measure of self-respect and control over their own finances, though they are not a panacea for all credit ills. Many remain under-resourced, and a funding initiative is urgently needed, perhaps a charity or trust fund, to provide 'seed' money for new community credit unions, as well as funds for training and resource material.

But they can serve a more direct commercial purpose than

simply escape from debt nightmares. The mixture of savings and loans by a mutual organisation suits members of a close-knit community who want to raise large sums to start in business or for big purchases, but have the cashflow to service the loans and the inclination to save at the same time. Thus one of the largest credit unions, with £1 million in assets, is run by and for London taxi drivers, while another typically was recently founded by Tyneside's Enterprise 5 Housing Association. A pump-priming role by government, by greatly expanding credit unions, could greatly enhance financial opportunities for millions with little or no capital. Significantly the US has some 160,000 credit unions with 54 million members, while the UK has only 241 credit unions with only 164,000 members. Moreover the vast majority of the latter are in Northern Ireland, where a strong and well-organised League of Credit Unions has achieved 300 times the market penetration of Great Britain.

A Poll Grant

Another valuable means of spreading financial opportunity throughout the population would be via a more equal allocation of capital resources at the start of working life. It fits a market model whereby everyone begins with roughly equal endowment of resources and all goods and resources are then allocated by competitive markets. The state's role would involve severe restrictions on the transfer of wealth, whether based on the socialist principle of egalitarianism or the capitalist goal of meritocracy.

At present, wealth is inherited extremely unequally and confers enormously unequal opportunities in early working life. The richest 1 per cent of adults in the UK, about a quarter of a million people, own 23 per cent of total marketable wealth, which represents an average holding per person of about £1.5 million in 1990. Their investment income in 1990 was £5 billion a year, nearly one-sixth of the nation's whole investment income, averaging £20,000 per person in this group. Moreover, it is wealth, not merit, which transmits this pattern through the generations. A study of inheritance by Harbury and Hitchens in 1979 found that three-fifths of rich men and three-quarters of rich women came themselves from rich families.

A modest recycling of this excessively skewed distribution of wealth could within a few years transform career openings for millions of people. A 3 per cent annual capital levy on the richest 3 per cent in Britain – those with net capital assets of more than £200,000 – would yield enough money to give more than £4,000 to every person on reaching their 21st birthday (about 900,000 each year), provided they could show they were putting it to some approved productive investment. However it was used (and consultative advice on how it might best benefit each individual in his or her own circumstances should be made freely available), it could provide for thousands the financial springboard they would otherwise never acquire. It might be called a citizen grant, or perhaps better – in ironic reversal of the deliberate inequity of the poll tax – it might be named a poll grant.

Capital Funds for the Workers

Another option for redistributing capital wealth more widely throughout the population – other than simply taxing it (certainly justified when capital taxes currently form only 3 per cent of total government tax revenue) – is by giving employees direct access to the build-up of capital holdings. This could be achieved in at least two main ways: through allocating a share in the profits to employees prior to the dividend distribution to the shareholders, and through the accumulation of employee-controlled capital funds in industry.

Offering workers a share in the profits is not new. ESOPS schemes are already fashionable, particularly in the US, but they suffer from two serious drawbacks: the proportion of the equity offered to workers (compared to top management) is often tiny, and they are exercised more as a handle to secure compliance than as an opening to extend power. Yet offering workers a genuinely significant slice in the profits yields substantial benefits for the company as well as for its employees. It ties the workforce into the success of the company as no exhortation could ever do: no profits, no bonus. And it gives the workforce a big incentive not to press for the maximum wage increase it can get away with, but the best trade-off between a somewhat lower wage increase and a much bigger capital bonus. Certainly the Japanese precedent of a 13th month capital pay-out to employees, dependent on the

previous year's success of the company, does not suggest the idea
is wasted as a corporate stimulus. It certainly enhances employee
loyalty and identification with the company, but the price for the
company is significant capital redistribution.

A variant on this idea is the build-up of capital funds in
industry collectively controlled by employees. Again there are
foreign models for this. In America, for example, a number of
unions together own 14 per cent of Texas Instruments, the
fast-growing semi-conductor manufacturer, and other major US
companies like McDonalds, Delta Air Lines and Holiday Inns
show similar patterns. In Sweden, wage earner funds have been
systematically year by year amassing increasing control over the
whole range of Swedish industry. They offer several pointers for
the development of union-controlled pension funds in the UK.
They are organised on a regional basis, they are deliberately
established with substantial worker control, they share the
benefits of profitability, and they are the exclusive property of the
workers.

This by no means exhausts the range of new mechanisms
which can be devised to extend real financial power within a
market economy to ordinary people. It is a principle which should
unremittingly be pursued further as every financial innovation
opens up novel opportunities to disseminate power among wider
groupings.

12

Dispersing Power
to Make the Economy Efficient

Redistributing power so that people can exercise real control over
each of the main institutions that affect their lives may be a
desirable goal. But is it compatible with the harsh disciplines of
economic policy required for the competitive success on which
everyone's living standards depend?

The object of economic policy must be a long-term sustainable
growth rate which steadily increases living standards while
minimising both the level of unemployment and the rate of
inflation. It is a goal which has eluded Britain, not only in the
de-regulated market of the last decade, but in a century of
uninterrupted decline relative to other nations since 1870. For any
government, reversing that decline must have the highest
priority. How practical then are the fundamental power reforms
advocated in this book – would they hamper the dictates of
economic policy and therefore have to be jettisoned, or might they
actually assist them?

What is Wrong with the British Economy?

In the quarter century of strong post-war growth in Western
capitalism 1948–73, the symptoms of Britain's profound loss of
competitiveness became painfully manifest in 1955 at the first
stop-go-stop cycle. The deflationary brake pushed unemployment to 0.4 million. At the trough of each successive cycle the
deflationary impact required to pull back spiralling trade deficits
and inflation became ever more severe. Unemployment rose to
0.6 million in 1961, to 1.0 million in 1971, to 1.3 million in 1978, to
3.1 million in 1985 and perhaps to 3.5 million in 1992.

The causes of this steady atrophying of Britain's competitive edge have been variously attributed according to political predilection. They have been sought in the dominance of the interests of the City of London over the needs of manufacturing, the excessive power of the unions and/or a generally poor quality of management, the rigidity of a class system which inhibited the rise of new talent and the development of innovation, over-centralised state controls that restricted market disciplines, chronic neglect of training both of the workforce and management, and long-term low investment levels – a list of culprits that is far from exhaustive.

Some remedies, again reflecting mainly political targeting, have been applied. Union power was decisively rolled back in the 1980s and managerial quality gradually improved, though surveys suggest it is still significantly inferior to the German, Japanese and US competition. The Thatcher era pushed through mass de-regulation of almost all economic controls. Yet other fundamental problems remain untackled. City financial interests still override the needs of manufacturing, even though the financial and service sectors remain far too small to compensate for manufacturing weakness in the balance of payments. The British class system still inhibits flexibility in a far from open and meritocratic society. The supply-side mechanisms of a market economy – training, R&D, technology introduction, public investment in infrastructure and private investment in manufacturing innovation – remain chronically deficient.

If post-war experience shows that there is one mistake to be avoided in economic policy, it is the belief that there is a mono-causal explanation of decline and therefore a single panacea. In the 1950s attention focused on the macro-economic problems of fine-tuning demand; in the 1960s on the range of micro-economic factors holding down productivity; in the 1970s on strikes and destructive industrial relations; and in the 1980s on privatisation and de-regulation. Each of these 'fashionable' solutions was at least in part a response to genuine concerns. But each was also pursued with single-minded disregard of other elements in the mosaic, and by trying to solve one issue at the expense of exacerbating others. A sensible economic policy must therefore keep in train simultaneously a whole set of targets without letting any single ideological obsession dominate.

Decentralising economic power has a major role to play, but it would be wrong to see it as another single panacea.

Overcoming the Trade Constraint

Monetarists argued that the solution to Britain's poor growth and productivity performance lies in improving the functioning of the supply side of the economy, to promote flexibility and change, and that this could be achieved whilst inflation was being reduced by restrictive monetary policies. In fact, when it was tried 1979–82, the effect was a severe acceleration in Britain's long-term de-industrialisation: 25 per cent of the country's manufacturing capacity was wiped out in the worst recession since World War II. Nor did it lay the foundation for the long boom of 1984–9. That was not launched by improvements in the supply side, but by unleashing an inflationary credit boom through removing virtually all controls on bank lending.

The 'expansionists' (the Keynesian National Institute and the Cambridge Economic Policy Group) have argued on the other hand that a more rapid expansion of aggregate demand is a necessary condition for better performance, so long as it led to higher output rather than to inflation. But while such demand management policies seemed to work as expected in the 1950s and 1960s, they broke down in the 1970s. With increased world wide inflation and the move to floating exchange rates, boosting domestic demand increased inflation much more than output. The National Institute, which sees the fundamental problem and its solution as lying in the labour market, has since argued for a permanent incomes policy. But a practicable version has yet to be designed.

The Cambridge Group, which regards the external trade constraint as the crucial element, has advocated general import controls partly to counter the initial inflationary effects of downward movements in the exchange rate, and partly to improve the structure of demand, so that the stimulus leads to a balanced expansion. They argue strongly that the scheme is not protectionist so long as it is used not to improve our balance of payments, but to increase domestic output and employment. In other words, any such scheme must be combined with an expansionary monetary and fiscal stance such that domestic output and employment are raised so much that imports as a whole are not lower than they otherwise would have been. If this condition were fulfilled, the rest of the world, taken as a whole, would not suffer at all and might well benefit, so there would be no grounds for retaliation.

It is an issue of central concern when UK competitiveness has deteriorated to the point where in 1990–1 output fell 4 per cent and unemployment rose by 0.75 million, yet the balance of payments remained stubbornly in deficit by as much as £13 billion (over 2 per cent of GDP). Another dash for growth would assuredly be broken very quickly on the rocks of subsequent retrenchment required to correct a trade imbalance that would rapidly become insupportable at 4–6 per cent of GDP (especially since covering the trade gap by the export of assets, which might have been possible in the early 1980s when Britain's total overseas assets exceeded £140 billion, is no longer possible in the early 1990s by which time they have shrunk to less than £30 billion). Yet only sustained growth, in excess of 3 per cent a year, can bring down unemployment from its 3 million plateau and fund the rise in public expenditure needed to repair crumbling schools, hospitals, housing, road and rail systems, and urban dereliction.

Essentially the country faces three options. One is to expand the economy, in a manner designed to minimize a rush of imports, by switching the bias in the engine of expansion away from exclusive reliance on tax cuts to a more balanced emphasis on public expenditure increases. For the same given expenditure, research (by Ormerod and Holland) shows that the latter produces roughly six times more jobs than the latter. It would also yield important supply-side gains by rebuilding deteriorated public sector capital stock. And it would keep down the marginal propensity to import following a rise in consumer expenditure, which some studies have shown is now as high as 80 per cent.

Even so, the balance of payments constraint would still rapidly apply. It would then be met by imposing a limit on the growth of imports at a point high enough so that the overall volume of imports over the next two to three year period remained at least as great as if it had been permitted to rise unchecked, but then had to be cut back by deflating domestic demand. That would still allow domestic output and employment to continue to grow up to the limit of the productive potential of the economy. The objections to such a policy however are that it is not a politically feasible option thus to break the letter of the Treaty of Rome (even though by maintaining or even increasing the volume of trade, it would not breach the spirit of the Treaty). There is also the technical problem that at the micro-economic level it would be difficult to treat different imports even-handedly.

A second option would be a similar expansionary stimulus, but based on a significant devaluation of the exchange rate in order to get the economy back on a sustainable growth path. That implies a fall of 10–15 per cent to a rate within the ERM of some DM 2.50–2.65 to the £. Even that, like the first option, still requires a sustained effort to improve the *real* supply side.

The third option would be to forego any direct expansion of the economy, and to rely exclusively on substantial improvements in the supply side to stimulate the economy out of recession. The overriding objection to that is that growth would be so inhibited that recovery from the fall in output and employment would politically be intolerably slow.

What is therefore needed is a controlled (and not initially excessive) stimulus for steady expansion of the economy, combined with *both* a substantial devaluation *and* sustained pressure for continuing supply-side improvements. The latter must include a huge expansion in both quantity and quality of training, a steady rise in R&D and its more thorough follow-through in technological innovation, an increase in investment to internationally competitive levels, and a regional policy to achieve better overall economic balance. Only if *all* these elements are set in place can there be hope of bringing unemployment down below the 1 million mark which last prevailed in the mid-1970s. *And getting unemployment below that level must be the unequivocal priority for economic policy* if spreading economic (and other) power throughout the population is to be the essence of the socialist approach.

Generating Minimum-inflation Growth

But even if the trade constraint can be contained, long-term growth sufficient to boost real incomes and abolish large-scale unemployment still faces the further barrier of being knocked off course by a splurge of inflation. There are several scenarios, all of which have been experienced in the recent period – government over-heating the economy through excessive public-sector reflation (the Barber dash for growth, 1973), wage cost-push pressure (union militancy, 1978–9), and excessive private-sector reflation following bank de-regulation (the Lawson credit boom, 1985–9).

What is needed is a new agenda for pay determination. Both employers and unions should accept that the style of pre-ERM wage bargaining, with pay deals based around a backward-looking measure of retail price inflation, is no longer feasible. The correct inflation rate to bargain around is the lowest expected average rate of wage inflation in the ERM. This forward-looking estimate should be made by a new and independent forecasting body, a Council of Economic Advisers, before the autumn wage round. The incentive for companies not to leap-frog would be further enhanced if the annual wage round were compressed into a much shorter period, preferably between the autumn statement and the budget.

It may however be said that this is over-ambitious and would simply not hold. An alternative prescription, which would still bear down strongly on wage inflation but would be more likely to secure co-operation across the board, would comprise two parts. First, unions and management would bargain over a feasible real wage increase (or reduction) for the coming year. They would bear in mind that in a year of around zero average productivity growth, any increase in the average real wage would cut jobs and undermine competitiveness. Then, second, they would add on the expected inflation rate; but if this expectation turned out to be too low, employees would then be compensated at agreed intervals to preserve the negotiated real wage.

That still leaves two other issues. One is that co-ordinated pay along these lines must be combined with decentralised bargaining so that wage differentials reflect local market conditions. That should be secured by the whole company bargaining procedures at plant level advocated in Chapter 5. *This shows again how the dispersal of power, in this case in the forum of pay determination, can help to promote efficiency as well as equity.*

The other issue is the choice of the rate of inflation. Since UK competitiveness will continue to deteriorate so long as the underlying inflation in the open sectors of the UK economy remains above that in Germany, the best forward-looking index to choose should be the expected German rate of inflation. This proposal would be advantageous to *both* workers and employers. If the German benchmark were used, workers would still not lose because their real wage would be guaranteed by the wage contract. On the other hand, companies must gain in aggregate since the alternative of paying workers in accordance with the backward-looking headline rate of inflation would involve a severe profit squeeze. By switching to such a contract the rate of increase of nominal wages and therefore UK prices would fall faster, because the expectation of German-style inflation would in part be self-fulfilling.

This policy would be enhanced further, to the mutual benefit of both workers and the economy, by the introduction of another element into this framework. Sharing a significant proportion of the annual profits with the workforce could play a big role in breaking the persistent unemployment/inflation dilemma. One option would be to pay a Japanese-style 'thirteenth month' salary as a bonus at the end of the year, depending on the last year's profits or some other productivity criterion. So long as the bonus is potentially large enough, it gives workers an in-built interest in efficient working and moderate pay claims.

Another option is to write revenue-sharing firmly into the wage contract, similarly to the proposal popularised by Martin Weitzman of MIT. Instead of employees being rewarded purely by pay, they would receive a mix of slightly lower pay plus a share of the surplus. Thus if instead of receiving a wage of (say) £8 an hour, an employee received a base wage of £7 an hour plus 20 per cent of the gross operating profits of £5 an hour (that is, average value-added per worker of £12 minus the £7 basic wage), he would still get £8 an hour, but two very beneficial economic results would follow. The firm has an incentive to absorb more of the unemployed because with only seven-eighths of additional revenue per extra employee going in pay, it will recruit extra workers so long as their revenue-generating contribution exceeds £8 an hour, instead of £12 in the pure wage case. The second result, and the relevant one here, is that employees have a strong incentive to restrain their own wage demands if by so doing they can gain more in their share of the capital surplus generated.

Making the Supply Side Competitive for Long-term Growth

If growth is not to break down under pressure from a mounting trade deficit and/or from a rising inflationary spiral, the supply side of the economy must at least match the efficiency of competitor countries. In the Thatcherite decade emphasis was concentrated for this purpose on privatisation, de-regulation, competitive tendering of public services, the systematic under-mining of trade-union power, and the application of commercial criteria throughout government and the public sector. What was lacking, because of a dogmatic hostility to the public sector, was development of non-market mechanisms which are necessary to underpin long-term success, but which in market terms would not yield short-term profit.

The foundations of sustainable economic prosperity lie in competitive levels of investment, competitive civil R&D, high-quality training, balanced regional development, constant innovation in new technology, and an efficient transport infra-structure, as well as a competitive and broadly stable exchange rate, higher quality management, and a stricter competition policy against market dominance. All were seriously neglected in the 1980s. How should they be secured for the 1990s?

Achieving adequate investment in manufacturing plant (still in 1991 well below its real level a dozen years before), R&D, and new technology requires more than new tax incentives to private business. They would certainly help to offset the perennial UK investment problems of high interest charges on loan capital, a low net rate of return, and the counter-attraction of gilt-edged or property as a relatively risk-free alternative. But after repeated stop-go-stop episodes since World War II, industry lacks confidence that growth and investment will not be choked off as soon as it gets under way.

What is needed are new instruments that achieve a better balance between demand and supply so that the productive capacity of the economy can grow at optimal pace. To secure better demand management, two major new policy initiatives are required.

One is to provide an adequate flow of medium and long-term funds to industry at rates that match those available to our main competitors. The City claims there is no lack of funding, only a dearth of worthwhile investment projects. But a major reason for fewer investment initiatives is the excessive cost of initial finance, with real rates of interest often 5–7 per cent above those ruling in the G7 and most of the EEC. The structural solution to this problem is to shift towards the German–Japanese system of much closer banking involvement in industry with long-term finance backing that commitment, rather than the Anglo-Saxon stock-exchange system of arms-length transactions requiring a short-term payback. But in the meantime while high real interest rates prevail – though the more sensible fiscal policies advocated here in pages 153–5 would reduce the need for that – a new public sector role makes good sense for a national investment bank to lend to approved additional manufacturing projects at rates broadly competitive with those abroad, with public subsidies to match the difference.

The other requirement to restore an effective role to demand management is a reversal of the de-regulation of financial markets in the mid-1980s which generated the inflationary credit boom and led directly to the prolonged and deep recession of 1989–92. The uncontrolled and explosive surge in private bank lending after the removal of all controls did as much damage in inflation and trade deficits in the 1980s as an over-expanded public sector borrowing requirement did in the 1970s. Reserve asset ratios for deposits with the central bank, 'full funding' techniques for government debt, and the 'corset' (which sets targets for the growth of the banking system's deposits) were all sensible ways to control the growth of credit, operated widely throughout the EEC, but foolishly abandoned by the Thatcher government in favour of controlling the money supply, which then proved unworkable. All three procedures, which are of proven worth, should be restored.

But in addition it is essential that renewed Keynesian demand management should now be supplemented by *supply management*. At present, production and investment decisions are isolated, with decision-makers in each company trying to decide in the light of what they believe everyone else is likely to do. Investment decisions are never co-ordinated and there is no collective responsibility for them. Each firm individually therefore tends to be over-cautious for fear of being caught out by another stop-go as the results of any new investment come on stream. A unified understanding on the basis of which all move forward together never emerges.

The planning framework required is a system of negotiated accords between government and leaders in the main corporate sectors whereby if the former reflates the economy by so much, then the latter for their part will expand their production, and if need be increase their investment, by about the same degree. There would of course have to be close consultations about the exact degree that was appropriate in any particular case, but the broad aim would be to ensure that the *overall* result accorded with the government's aim of (say) a 3 to 4 per cent reflation with minimum inflationary repercussions. For the first time machinery to secure a steady and controlled growth of output matching a given stimulation of demand would fine-tune expansion between, on the one hand, too little increase in output because of leakage into inflation and, on the other, overheating the economy because of excess growth of demand.

High-quality training, balanced regional development, and an efficient transport infrastructure must be treated, not as a public expenditure burden or a PSBR cost, but as a critically necessary *investment*. In all three, Britain starts the last decade of the twentieth century far below comparable European levels of provision of its main Franco–German competitors, at levels amongst the lowest in the EEC, and having fallen markedly further behind in the previous Thatcherite decade. A steady increase in national investment in these three areas is not therefore an incubus on market growth, but a necessary condition of its realisation. In particular, employers should be statutorily required to undertake the regular upgrading of the skills of their workforce at least to a minimum percentage of payroll (say, initially, 1 per cent). Non-trainers who poach or those whose training does not offer the requisite standard should have to make a default payment for others – good practice employers or public skill-centres – to provide the high-quality training that Britain now desperately needs.

Re-industrialising Britain

Sustained growth and a long-term fall in unemployment still require three further conditions, in addition to these supply-side improvements. One is a major and lasting shift from consumption to investment. What was so perverse about the Lawson boom 1985–9 was not that it caused total demand to rise too fast, nor even that the excessive growth of total demand caused inflationary pressure, but that a vastly higher proportion of resources than ever before went into personal consumption and into services and property.

By the end of 1988 the level of household indebtedness had reached a staggering £300 billion, equal to about the entire annual flow of disposable income. Indeed the *growth* of indebtedness during the single year 1988 was no less than £54 billion. By 1989 it was clear that a necessary condition for achieving sustained growth in the future was that personal consumption over the next few years be held back by a large amount, probably about 8 per cent below trend, and that a very large improvement in investment and net exports take up the slack. The slump of 1990–1, however painful, was no greater than was necessary for this purpose. Even so, the fall in the growth of net household borrowing by an incredible £22 billion over the two-year period to the end of 1990 was unprecedented.

What did not happen, and what is still necessary, is that this huge fall in consumption be matched by a sustained and substantial rise in net export demand, that is, in exports relative to import penetration, plus a marked rise in investment in tradable goods and services. This was shown starkly by a visible trade deficit in 1991 stuck at £6 billion *even when the recession was in full swing with unemployment over 2.5 million and rising fast.*

A second main requirement for sustainable growth and long-term reduction in unemployment is a major switch in national budgeting in favour of manufacturing and away from arms spending, overseas investment and City priorities. For only a vigorous and competitive manufacturing base can produce the economic and financial weight, in a way that the much smaller service sector cannot match, to sustain the living standards of the nation offered by the level of imports sought.

Defence expenditure, at an annual £21 billion in 1989 was 4.1 per cent of GDP, about 1 per cent higher than the average for the European countries in NATO, an excess expenditure on defence by Britain of more than £5 billion a year. Even more significantly, after the collapse of the Berlin Wall in 1989 and the disintegration of the Soviet bloc over the next two years, continued defence spending at or near these levels clearly cannot be justified. Equally an immediate and huge 'peace dividend' may not be practicable, but in the course of the first half of the 1990s a steady reduction to one half or one third of these levels should still be consistent with fully safeguarding the country against any conceivable military attack in the post-Cold War international environment. That should allow an annual flow of £10 billion or more by the mid-1990s to be transferred to industrial or services investment, initially concentrated on arms conversion in areas of currently high defence employment.

Overseas investment following the removal of exchange controls in 1979 has leapt ahead from £7 billion to £31 billion in 1988. What is more disturbing is that direct (as opposed to portfolio) investment in industrial plant and equipment has surged from £6 billion in 1979 to £21 billion in 1988. In other words, pension and insurance funds and trans-national companies have been investing their surpluses much more heavily abroad than in the UK, promoting the growth of foreign output and employment much more than British. While a spread of overseas investments is no doubt prudent, the scale of under-funding of the weakened UK manufacturing base cannot be tolerated, when especially it becomes self-reinforcing over time. A better balance between home and foreign investment in manufacturing should therefore be secured by guidelines to investors which set ceilings on outlays overseas beyond which a sliding tax scale will be imposed in the UK. Such devices to 'repatriate' capital from abroad should provide the additional investment source to begin to close the serious investment gap in manufacturing between Britain and its main competitors.

Prioritising the City must also change if the long-term growth of output and jobs is to prevail. The City must not be allowed to override, with its prejudice for a strong pound, euphemistically called 'sound finance', a genuinely competitive exchange rate by which manufacturing can deliver steadily rising output and employment. The City of London remains the most lightly regulated international financial centre in the world, ostensibly in Britain's interest because it enhances the attractiveness of London as a financial marketplace; yet the gains to the UK balance of payments from 'invisibles' receipts dwindled to almost nothing during 1990–1 and were far outweighed by the constant haemorrhaging of net direct investment abroad. Moreover, since Big Bang in 1986 the City has focused largely on the international Eurodollar markets and has increasingly neglected the financial needs of domestic industry. On all these three counts – a lower exchange rate, re-regulation of financial markets and concentration on British industrial needs first – policy needs to be changed if manufacturing is to prevail in Britain.

The third requirement to revitalise British industry is to secure an adequate supply of medium to long-term funds at a cost broadly comparable to that for competitors abroad. At present, British firms are seriously disadvantaged on several counts. First, much less is invested in Britain. Britain's commercial and industrial companies' net investment is about 4 per cent of GDP; by comparison, Japan normally invests about 12 per cent net, and France and Germany around 8 per cent. Second, in Britain around 70 per cent of investment capital comes from within industry itself; the German entrepreneur is able to raise nearly three times as much money from the banks as the British. In Britain bank loans to industry amount to some 3 per cent of GDP, compared with 8 per cent for Germany and 15 per cent for Japan. Third, Japan's industrialists have really long-term loans of 15–20 years, and in Germany the formal term averages 7 years; in Britain it is 2.5 years, though roll-over can increase this. Fourth, German managers can borrow up to two-thirds of their company assets, but British managers will not be advanced more than one-third. And German banks will value the assets as part of a going concern, while British banks will look only at their break-up value.

Tackling these drawbacks in Britain requires major policy changes. There are basically three options. One is for the government to lay down guidelines for portfolio allocation for the pension and insurance funds, that is, at least a significant proportion (for example a third) to be devoted to approved manufacturing projects in the UK. After all, the existing rule giving absolute discretion to fund managers to maximise their investment returns is neither in the interests of the UK if it leads to extensive investment abroad nor historically has it produced more than mediocre returns in practice. Another option is for the government to take over one of the Big Four commercial banks in order to set a new pattern, which the others would be obliged to follow, in direct and sustained involvement in industry. A third option is to set up a national investment bank, as a subsidiary of the Bank of England, channelling savings into productive industry in the form of long-term loans of up to 20 years' maturity, or equity finance for small and medium-size enterprises.

Partnership with Industry: the Relationship with the TNCs

Even all these policies for supply-side revival and for the general re-industrialisation of Britain will still not suffice if either the industrial leadership, structure of production or technological application is not up to the competition. A London Business School study by Stopford and Turner in the mid-1980s found that too many leading British companies (for example Pilkington, EMI and Sinclair) lacked the vision and controlled commercial aggression that drives the best Japanese and American companies to combine technological excellence and global ambition with strength in distribution and all the other dimensions of a leadership strategy.

British companies are heavily skewed towards low-technology industries like tobacco, drink, building materials, paper, textiles and hotels where competition is tougher than in the newer, highly research-intensive industries. They tend to be poorly structured and excessively reliant on growth by acquisition rather than on fundamental investment in better product design. And too many British companies still have the illusion they are technological leaders when, with honourable exceptions like ICI and pharmaceuticals, real rates of UK spending on R&D have been dropping over the past decade.

Restructuring of production is clearly needed to create key national strengths – Britain lacks for example a consumer electronics business the size of Philips or a telecommunication enterprise the size of Ericsson, and has no big international car maker. But that will require much more flexible management of industrial change as industry constantly restructures itself, using Japanese systems to re-deploy workers from declining sectors to growing ones. Indeed, Japanese success has rested on maintaining constant pressure on three major fronts – reducing costs, increasing overseas production and stepping up product development. For much better exploitation of British inventiveness, what is needed is a public-sector innovation agency offering technical, managerial and financial assistance (on strictly commercial assessments) to promote the funding, production and marketing of new products.

Another part of the new framework required for the re-industrialisation of Britain is the creation of key industrial regions where the active collaboration of government and business can build up a 'public sphere'. That would embrace common services, the generalisation of best practice in the region or industry as a whole, mutual assistance between firms, sustained relationships of trust with vital sub-contractors, and co-operation to promote the collective upgrading of the skills of the labour force. Britain should emulate these elements of an industrial 'public sphere' which are strongly present among our most successful competitors, most notably in Emilia-Romagna in Italy and Baden-Wurttemburg in Germany.

But collaboration between government and industry needs to be built on some formal basis of mutual rights and obligations. It has been one of the central themes of this book that as a result of the systematic application of micro-chip technology throughout industry and society, there has been a fundamental shift in the Western economies in the last two decades towards flexible, customised manufacturing and a decentralised economy. While however this has led to a huge expansion of small-scale enterprise and part-time working, it has also been accompanied by a still greater concentration of size and power among the biggest companies which are the industrial leaders in each sector.

Ensuring that they respond to government plans for external restructuring and the internal democratic power-sharing agenda requires, because of their dominant position within the economy, a special framework. Development agreements between government and sector leaders – on the model widely used by European countries like France and Belgium and to some extent in Japan – should cover key sectoral business planning for future output, employment, investment, exports and import substitution, as well as training and the employee opportunity agenda. In certain sectors there is a strong case also for public ownership of one of the key industrial leaders, whether to ensure the mechanics of regulation fully effective (for example pharmaceuticals) or to shift financial activity in new directions (for example banking).

A New Role for Trade Unions

No economic policy can fully succeed which does not wholly harness the commitment and loyalty of its workforce to its central objectives. That means shifting steadily away from the classic Victorian joint-stock enterprise, which buys and sells its workers in a marketplace like its commodities, to the *community model firm* which seeks and gives loyalty and trust. In the former, bargaining is normally by skill or craft and is adversarial. The pay is the rate for the particular job, and bosses can put their own pay up even when they are sacking workers. Labour turnover is high, differentials are great and so are rivalries. Bosses fear their deputies are after their job and they are right. Conditions of work, like different canteens and toilets, divide the workforce. Relatively little training is done because the individual may then move, so the company does not benefit.

In the community model firm, for which paradoxically Japan provides a precedent, bargaining is with an enterprise union across the plant so that the workforce shares a common interest. Pay depends on gradings within the same occupation and on the success and prestige of the concern, probably with profit-sharing or a bonus scheme. Facilities are shared. Seniority constrains the ability to promote quickly, which helps concentrate rivalries outside the firm rather than within it. Because people are hired to work for the organisation rather than as an engineer or fitter from the marketplace, training and learning is a continuous process. There is often lifetime employment. Managers work in open-plan offices and often take a pay cut if sacrifices need to be taken elsewhere. They think long-term because they will be there long-term and so will their bankers.

Clearly in terms of classical economics, the community model firm suffers from inefficiency in allocations – labour is immobile, markets are sticky and oligopoly rules. But this is far more than balanced by the fact that the social compensations – the compromises made in favour of people who would lose out from the free working of market forces, and the mobilising of a sense of obligation and personal commitment in employment relations – generates a sense of fairness which enables people to work co-operatively, conscientiously and with a will. It is a model which should form the centre-piece of industrial strategy and the objective for trade union action.

Trade unions have traditionally been built around the conflict model and equipped to fight the major set-piece action. The macho-management style of the 1970s and 1980s was met by macho-trade union confrontation. Such tactics however are of dwindling relevance to a labour force where two out of every three jobs will soon be provided in the service sector. At the end of the 1980s, 8 per cent of jobs created in one year were taken by men working full-time, while 42 per cent were taken by women working part-time and 18 per cent by women working full-time. In that year, about 340,000 net jobs were created in service industries, while 130,000 jobs were lost in manufacturing.

An entirely new approach is therefore required if unions are to meet the needs of employees in the 1990s in a fast-changing labour market driven by the new information technologies. The old-style massive, remote, impersonal, conflict-oriented, hierarchical, male-dominated trade union structure has had its day. The accent must now be on a much more flexible, close, personalised approach for dealing with problems. For the purpose may be to represent members in local heterogeneous bargaining situations, or to advise them on health and safety risks which are not standardised, or to negotiate needed services like flexible hours, creche facilities or cancer screening, or to represent part-time workers with irregular hours and high turnover, or to negotiate training schedules that are tailor-made for the individual, or even to assist unemployed ex-members to get back into work. The list is long and very varied.

Such a new role will require a big increase in union resources wholly differently directed (though the TGWU Link-up campaign, among others, shows re-direction is under way). That will then require a big increase in membership fees, now at a historically very low level, to be justified by a substantially improved service package. It will also require new structures to reflect the new priorities: for example COHSE has an 85 per cent female membership in nursing but only one female national officer, while the TGWU as the biggest general union has a total of 1.3 million members but less than 0.2 million female members, though women will within five years constitute nearly half the workforce. Trade unions *are* increasingly pursuing women's issues – like job segregation, bonus schemes, and part-time workers' access to pension schemes – and there are gradually more women full-time officers, but they are still almost wholly excluded from main power positions. Yet only women in top positions will fully re-direct unions towards their new role for the future.

In summary, the new decentralised economy of the 1980s and 1990s can no longer be organised around monolithic large-scale planning, whether in the public or the private sector. It requires new instruments to reverse the long-standing failings of the British economy, notably the trade constraint on sustained growth, the inflation–unemployment see-saw, the supply-side weaknesses in manufacturing, the dominance of international finance over domestic re-industrialisation, and a damaging conflict model in industrial relations. There is no single panacea, but all these deep-seated problems can be addressed by a range of new solutions outlined here, all relatively inexpensive, yet likely to bring more people and more creative energies into play. In particular, a policy for dispersing power can make a new and unique contribution to the containment of inflation, more constructive industrial relations and a sustained improvement to supply-side performance.

13

Diffusing Power
in the New World Order

Power enfranchisement may offer a rich vision for the advancement of society in the industrialised world. But does it have relevance for the wider world stage?

The Current Pattern of International Power

People taking power to gain control over their own lives has always been the principle that inspired de-colonisations round the world, together with the strivings for democracy. The first has largely been realised as one by one the main imperial powers have been de-imperialised: the British by economic decline, the loss of empire and by Suez; the French by the loss of Indo-China and Algeria and also by Suez; the Germans, Japanese and Italians by their defeats in the World War II; the Americans by their retreat from Vietnam. Even the Confederation of Independent States (formerly the USSR), after Afghanistan and steady economic collapse at home, now confines its imperialism to its own restless republics. In many spheres of influence, however, direct political control has been replaced by economic imperialism.

The striving for democracy, on the other hand, still remains a dream over most of the globe. If a democracy is defined as 'a state whose central government was chosen by free and honest electoral process, open to candidates from rival political organisations, with reasonable opportunities to publicise their programmes', then of the 170 countries in the world, only some 46 can be described as genuinely democratic, covering about 34 per cent of the world's population. In addition, there are another 44 countries, embracing a further 20 per cent of the world's population, which are emerging, but not consolidated, democracies. So 2.5 billion people, almost half the world's population, continue to live under autocratic, and often tyrannical and bloodthirsty, regimes.

Against this background President Bush proclaimed in 1990 his New World Order. It had a single focus: the US riding high, exercising a unipolar hegemony after 40 years of a shared US–Soviet duopoly. Europe and Japan would acquiesce in, even hail, Washington's leadership, even dominance. The UN, contrary to all historic experience, would gladly dance to the tune of the American piper (never mind that the latter had not bothered paying his dues for quite some time). The turbulent Third World would willy-nilly submit its controversies and conflict to US arbitration.

But it was a thoroughly flawed concept. The US saw partnership with Europe and Japan as meaning the latter would shoulder more of the financial burden, while *they* saw it as access to greater consultation and co-decision-making. Despite US pretensions, no single player on the international stage today has such overwhelmingly disproportionate power as to police the world alone any longer. Above all, the yardstick by which the prowess of nations is measured is inexorably changing. We are rapidly moving from the territorial–military–political age into an economic–financial–technological age. The US, with its economic, budgetary and social shortcomings, will steadily lose political and ultimately also military clout. All the others stand to make relative gains.

One World and the Redrawing of International Economic Power

If that is the international power geometry of the 1990s, how can a fairer deal for the world's poor be achieved? It is not a problem that the West can continue to ignore as it did in the 1980s. Since 1980 the gap between the rich and poor nations of the world has been widening for the first time since the World War II; 200 million more people are now living in absolute poverty. In Latin America output has been rising at only 1 per cent a year, compared with 10 per cent for most of the 1970s. Since population has been increasing much faster, living standards have been falling sharply. Latin America's debt, which sparked the banking crisis of the early 1980s which seriously threatened the whole of the Western financial system, is still rising.

Several plans for a different model of world development, sponsored by internationally drawn committees headed by distinguished world figures, were published in the 1980s. Following the New International Economic Order promulgated by UNCTAD in the 1970s, the Brandt Committee produced 'North: South' in 1980 and then 'Common Crisis' in 1983. This was followed by the Socialist International's 'Global Challenge', chaired by Michael Manley, in 1985. Their weakness however was that they were all premised on a readiness by the rich countries, particularly the most powerful Group of Seven (G7), to adopt, however compelling the analysis, a redistributionist strategy. This, within the current institutional framework, they simply will not do beyond a marginal extent.

Bretton Woods in 1944 sealed US dominance in the world economy. It established the International Monetary Fund (IMF) whose major role was to provide support, subject to conditions, for members in balance of payments difficulties. Because the voting structure in the IMF gave the US the power to veto any proposal, it allowed one government effectively to police other countries' economies by making assistance conditional on adopting policies which reinforced its own power, since failure to obey the dictates of the Fund could result in exclusion from it and hence inability to meet international debts. Bretton Woods also adopted the dollar as the main form of international currency, which gave the US virtual control over world liquidity. Another major institution established then was the World Bank which was designed to develop the productive capacity particularly of the less developed countries (LDCs). But it was open only to members of the IMF, and again the US held effective control.

Remoulding the Institutions

If the Third World is ever to throw off grinding poverty in much of its populations, overcome economic domination by the West, and escape endless indebtedness to its rich suppliers, a series of institutional changes will be required to alter the current balance of world economic power. Above all it requires a fundamental role in restructuring the IMF and World Bank.

The first concerns the IMF's handling of trading deficits incurred in the process of development. At present, IMF funding is to correct only short-term deficits. Yet that is wholly inappropriate to an LDC which needs to import a wide range of goods, particularly intermediate and capital goods such as steel and machinery. If its ability to import such goods is permanently restricted to the level of its earnings from agricultural exports, development is bound to be slow and it may be almost impossible relatively to catch up with the West. Moreover, the Fund only received a third of the resources originally proposed in 1944, so the *right* of governments to make drawings also had to be limited. Further, the IMF imposed conditions on lending above 25 per cent of a member's quota, and money drawn from the Fund has to be repaid over a short period (two to three years), so long-term transformation of the economy is precluded.

This no-win situation for LDCs is built on a false premise – that responsibility for preserving a trading equilibrium rests wholly on debtor countries, despite the crippling burdens of development from a low base. In fact, countries holding a large unused surplus of foreign exchange are tying up currency that should be kept in circulation. What is therefore needed is a fundamental change in IMF rules, or maybe rather a new alternative institution replacing it. This would hold the trading accounts of all nations, and all governments would be allocated an initial quota of international currency. All countries running *either* debit *or* credit balances above a certain level would then pay an annual charge. But this new post-IMF institution – let us call it the International Trading Union – would be allocated enough funds to see any LDC through balance of payments deficits caused by long-term development needs without any Western dictat distorting domestic economies.

This fundamental change in international trade requires another one since it is incompatible with the choice of the dollar as international money. For a demand for dollars in excess of the US contribution to the Fund could wreck the system. What is needed therefore is a *new* international currency which would be accepted in settlement of international trade accounts, but which would be outside the control of any one nation. Only then can there be an assurance of sufficient world liquidity to meet the long-term industrial investment needs of the LDCs, so long as the industrialised OECD countries mutually accept the truth that balanced world development is not only in the interests of the LDCs, but of themselves. For just as the lack of regional policy in the UK, or in the EEC, suppresses the demand that would maintain growth or pull the UK out of a downturn, so impoverishment of the south of the world not only perpetuates absolute poverty among a third or more of mankind, but flattens the market for high-tech capital goods that would extend growth in the West and counter recession.

Cui Bono? New Rules for the World Bank

Equally the operation of the World Bank needs to be fundamentally changed. At present its Articles enjoin it to promote the growth of international trade by encouraging private foreign investment. Only if this is not forthcoming, it is laid down, should it provide resources itself. This private sector-led concept of world industrial development has used economic power to suit US interests, at huge cost to the LDCs themselves. It consolidated an open world trading system which worked to the advantage of the strongest economic power, which for 30 years after the World War II was the US, but produced lop-sided development according to the investment priorities and profit repatriation of trans-national companies.

What is needed is a World Bank dedicated to long-term LDC development (which *is* ostensibly its purpose), not the interest of the existing world economic super-powers. The criterion for both World Bank and IMF intervention should not be free market, that is, private sector-driven economics. In effect this has been used to deny international aid to socialist/communist countries and to try to force them towards the capitalist world trading bloc. It should be for LDCs themselves to choose the balance between their public and private sectors, and the Articles of the World Bank should be changed to respect this. Criteria for international aid should rigorously exclude political ideology. What they *should* take account of, to prevent abuse or corruption by recipient governments and to ensure their accountability to their own peoples, are three key factors: a code of basic human rights and civil freedoms, a readiness to move towards democratic institutions, and an international regime of arms control.

Of course it may be argued that prescribing such criteria for international money flows is not realistic when the existing economic super-powers will not allow the rules that favour them to be changed. However, several trends suggest it is far from impracticable. After the last world war the US accounted for half of world gross product, but now it is down to a quarter. World economic power is now tri-polar, and if Japan and the EEC exerted influence commensurate to their strength in 'their' economic spheres of Asia and Africa, a different pattern of international development could emerge.

Now that America in both its trading and budget deficits has become the world's largest debtor, the quotas to the IMF and World Bank should be re-drawn to reflect new economic realities and hence US control over development aid should be reduced, opening the way to establishing new criteria. What is needed is a transformation of the US-dominated World Bank into an economic version of the UN, open to all nations in accordance with their GNP-based quota contributions. The so-called Group of 77 LDCs (now expanded to over 120) have more leverage today than in the abortive UNCTAD negotiations in the 1960s and 1970s, and should use it to press the irrefutable demand that the world economy should reflect a level playing field, not one biased to preserve the interests of the most powerful.

Getting Trading Systems that Favour the LDCs

But more than simply demanding a fairer institutional system to govern the world economy, the LDCs should take power into their own hands. The IMF has traditionally offered more money and support to the north than the south; in the late 1970s for example, 62 per cent of all drawings went to industrialised countries, even though the south contributed 72 per cent of the money in the Fund, thus effecting a net transfer of purchasing power from south to north). Hence it is clear that such aid as is received by LDCs, hamstrung as it is too by conditionality, will never be sufficient for them to flourish in an open world economy. Instead they should set up trading systems that work to their own advantage, in particular integrated customs unions with other countries at their own level of development.

Contrary to much conventional wisdom in the West, association with an advanced trading bloc like the EEC can seriously damage an LDC. Reciprocal tariff reduction on all sides will not favour LDC interests because it will inhibit home industrialisation, limit the saving of foreign exchange for the purchase of input imports, and throw back LDCs on to over-reliance on the production of primary products in which they have a comparative advantage. It also leads to over-dependence on the terms of trade of these primary products which are notoriously volatile, and over-dependence on exports for which there is a limited demand. It biases LDC imports towards sophisticated Western high-tech products when what LDCs like India need most is an intermediate technology appropriate to their level of development and the availability of a huge unemployed or under-employed labour supply.

The domestic markets of LDCs are generally small, so there is little chance to produce import substitutes economically while the countries remain on their own. But through integration the member countries can agree to specialise and thus each provide a number of products for a much larger market so that economies of scale can be realised, but without their being swamped by the technological superiority of the advanced countries in the First World. Precedents like ASEAN in South-East Asia should be extended to sub-Saharan Africa and Central and Latin America. Efficient import substitution can then take place in products already made in at least one of the member countries, and possibly entirely new industries may become economical for the production of import substitutes for the whole group.

Debt Remission for a New Start

If LDCs are to take power to themselves to lay real foundations for their own prosperity and to escape persisting thraldom to the old colonial powers, it requires three conditions to be fulfilled. None of them is a big increase in aid provision which, however welcome in itself, would simply perpetuate LDCs' fundamental underlying dependence and fail to tackle the causes of their economic subordination. The first two conditions already outlined are not enough by themselves – a reformulation of the voting power, composition and objectives of the IMF and World Bank which the G77 should demand in a recalled Bretton Woods conference, and the establishment of integrated customs unions suited to LDC development levels, not as adjuncts to industrialised powers' trading patterns.

The third requirement is a significant measure of debt forgiveness, without which many LDCs stand little chance of emerging from economic disaster. World Bank figures show that in 1989 debt in sub-Saharan African countries represented 93 per cent of GDP and debt service accounted for 21 per cent of exports of goods and services. In some Latin American countries the export earnings to debt service ratio rose even higher, to 28 per cent in the case of Mexico and 42 per cent of Argentina. By 1989 debt-rescheduling countries owed $520 billion to private creditors, plus a further similar amount to official creditors (more than double the figure for only six years before). By 1991 the total debt burden had risen to a staggering $1,341 billion. The total *net* transfer of resources from all debtor countries to the creditor countries, the reverse flow from poor to rich, rose to a crippling $43 billion a year.

After the dam against debt remission was first breached at the Toronto economic summit in 1988, the Brady initiative in 1989 encouraged Western banks to forgive debts, while in 1990 the write-off of two-thirds of certain official debt was proposed under the Trinidad terms. Then Poland, which owed three-quarters of its $40 billion debt to Western governments, was afforded remission of 80 per cent of its debt.

Official debt forgiveness has however only been made available to those countries following 'sound' economic policies approved by the IMF. This is as short-sighted and counter-productive as the EBRD's constitution in 1991 limiting lending to countries 'applying the principles of multi-party democracy, pluralism and market economics'. It is an attempt to impose ideological domination in a global economy which is morally untenable and politically divisive. There are two strong reasons why the industrial countries should grant the Third World a much higher level of debt remission than has yet been agreed. One is that Western governments are largely responsible for the debt plight of many LDCs because of their policy during the 1970s of recklessly encouraging bank lending to the Third World. They did so for reasons of their own self-interest – to allow debtor countries to sustain their oil imports despite the OPEC price rises and thus avoid a more severe economic and trade recession for the world economy – and should now take responsibility for the consequences. The other reason is that the scale of LDC debt and debt servicing is so large that it seriously inhibits world economic growth, from which all parties lose. For not only are debtors themselves clearly worse off, but because they can only earn surpluses to make net transfers by depressing their imports, which cuts demand for industrial countries' goods, creditors lose too. The world economy is not a zero-sum game in which one person wins what another loses.

A New Stronger Role for the UN

New world economic institutions with a more balanced mandate, intra-LDC common markets suited to their own development levels, and widespread debt remission should be pursued by a combination of G77 demands organised in a new international forum, inter-LDC negotiations, and exploitation of industrial countries' self-interest. They should all enhance LDC power. But how can empowerment of their populations be pursued *within* LDCs?

The prime requirement is protection of basic human rights for all people in non-democratic societies liable to violation of individuals' freedom and suppression of minorities. Horrific examples abound over the last decade of internal repression of their own peoples by governments, or by occupying powers, including Pol Pot in Cambodia, Idi Amin in Uganda, the Indonesian army in East Timor, China in Tibet, India in Kashmir, Saddam Hussein against the Kurds in Iraq, Mengistu in Ethiopia, to name just some of the more extreme examples.

In the light of these murderous regimes, the post-war UN doctrine of non-interference in the domestic affairs of a sovereign country needs to be urgently reviewed. It should be overturned where there is clear evidence of the gravest violation of human rights – where genocide is being perpetrated or threatened by a government against its own people. In fact this is already accepted in the international community both de jure and de facto. The UN Genocide Convention 1948, though so far hardly used, explicity rules that 'persons committing genocide . . . shall be punished, whether rulers, public officials or private individuals'. In practice,

there was no international outcry when the Vietnamese overthrew Pol Pot or when Tanzania overthrew Idi Amin. Furthermore, interference in the domestic affairs of another country has
repeatedly been exercised by the US, notably in recent years in
Panama, Grenada and Nicaragua.

The UN should maintain a standing army with contingents in
different countries ready for rapid deployment. Where evidence
of mass violation of citizen rights amounting to genocide was
reported, the matter would be debated in full in the General
Assembly and a resolution passed calling on the offending
country to cease immediately the systematic extermination of
large sections of its own population, but if it failed to do so within
a stated timescale, then international force would be used to stop
it. This would give more protection to oppressed minorities than
has ever existed before (as well as reasserting the power of the UN
dormant since the death of Hammarskjold during UN military
intervention in the Congo in 1961). And it would extend a real
measure of power to the most powerless of all, those minorities
victimised by their own governments.

Additional international measures are needed to protect
individuals – dissidents, political opponents, trade union leaders,
teachers, human rights lawyers or simply citizens picked out at
random – in countries where torture is administratively routine.
The principle of non-interference in the domestic affairs of a third
country should certainly not be lightly discarded; equally
however it cannot lead to the grossest violations of the most basic
human rights being disregarded. If our goal is that people
worldwide should have power to control their own destiny,
action on this front is the most fundamental of all.

A system of multilateral sanctions should be operated under
UN auspices which would exert a cumulative array of pressures
against the worst offenders – withdrawal of arms supplies,
cessation of aid, discouragement of foreign investment, a ban on
bank loans and a range of trade sanctions (from withdrawal of
tariff preferences to limitations on purchases of key products from
the offending country, permitted under Article 113 of the Treaty
of Rome on grounds of 'public morality'). The UN should also
supervise an international exchange of information on torturers'
identities so that they are outlawed with no haven to protect them
against being brought to justice.

Another new role for the UN that is urgently needed concerns arms control. If Third World development is to be optimised in the interests of all its citizens, the ruinously expensive arms trade, on which so many elitist cliques spend an excessively high proportion of GNP to preserve their own power while keeping their own peoples impoverished, has to be rigorously controlled. The UN Development Programme estimated in 1991 that some £30 billion a year of misused money could be released for human development if Third World governments changed their spending priorities. For example, the health and education share of the national budget is less than a third of the military share in Iraq, Iran, Uganda, Oman, Pakistan, UAE, Angola, Peru and Chad.

The UN should take the lead in establishing a new regime for controlling the international arms trade regime. Countries that systematically and routinely torture their own citizens should be declared pariahs and denied all military aid. A ban of this kind should be enforceable in a semi-watertight manner when the Big Five nuclear powers – America, Britain, France, the CIS (formerly the USSR), and China – account for about 85 per cent of the exports of big military items such as tanks and artillery, radar and guidance systems, missiles and warships. Furthermore, military aid should be severely limited where (i) a country chooses to spend more on its military than on the education and health of its people, or (ii) a country has no democratic institutions so that its citizens have no say over budgetary priorities.

One other innovative role which only the UN can properly play concerns the protection of minorities, whether the Kurds or Shi'ites in Iraq, Armenians in the former USSR, Catholics in Northern Ireland, or blacks in Western societies, to name but a few. What is needed is a UN Charter of Fundamental Rights for Minorities which would detail a set of basic conditions designed to guarantee freedom from persecution, non-discrimination and rights of equal participation in public life.

Where these basic conditions were seriously breached and a report setting out the evidence was presented to the UN by leaders of the oppressed minority, the UN should send representatives to seek to verify the claims made. If confirmed (or where the offending government refuses access either partly or wholly), their findings plus the original report would be debated by the UN Assembly. If confirmation of the original allegations is endorsed by the vote, the UN should adopt a resolution setting out measures to be applied against the offending government according to the severity of persecution of the minority. These might include restraint on cultural or sporting contacts, reductions or cessation of aid programmes, withdrawal of ambassadors, breaking off diplomatic relations or (in extreme cases) a range of trade sanctions.

Filling the Democratic Deficit in the EEC

Another major application of the principle of power dispersal in the international arena concerns control of the European Economic Community. At present, the EEC is wholly undemocratic. Only the Commission, in effect a supra-national civil service, can introduce directives and other legislation. The Council of Ministers has powers going far beyond those of national cabinets, since the latter have ultimately to report to a parliament. The European parliament, the only element directly elected, has extremely limited powers which make it quite ineffective.

Until the mid-1980s member states retained ultimate control through the Council of Ministers and the principle of unanimous decision. Since the Single European Act of 1987 extended the principle of qualified majority voting, member states will sometimes have to accept decisions opposed by their own governments. So far, that applies mainly to economic and commercial measures; but in future it may well be extended to cover environmental and social matters. As this happens, national parliaments will gradually lose control over their own affairs. Already vital and sensitive issues like immigration, visa policy, asylum for refugees, extradition and cross-border co-operation between police forces are being decided by completely unaccountable committees like the Trevi Group, the Working Group on Immigration and the Co-ordinators Group. This failure to secure full accountability to European electors for decisions which have been taken away from domestic parliaments is the 'democratic deficit'.

Now that majority voting marks the crucial dividing line where national sovereignty gives way to supra-national power-sharing, accountability requires scrutiny by *both* national parliaments *and* by the European parliament. The previous democratic structure of the EEC, whereby member states' governments take decisions in the Council of Ministers and are accountable to their national parliaments for their actions, will no longer suffice. The radical extension of this should be to accord to the Euro-parliament the right to 'co-decision' – an equal say with the Council throughout the whole process of legislation, together with the right to initiate new legislation and the right to fire *individual* commissioners. Alternative proposals, like imposing a senate of national MPs on top of the elected Euro-parliament or reverting to the dual mandate whereby an MP can serve both in Westminster and Strasbourg, would be both cumbersome and impractical.

Another aspect of filling the democratic deficit must be the relentless application of 'subsidiarity'. In other words, only those decisions should be delegated to Brussels which strictly need to be delegated. All other decisions should be decentralised to the fullest extent feasible, whether to the national state or to the region.

The EEC project however is a dynamic one, and as progress is made towards stages two and three of the Delors plan for Economic and Monetary Union (EMU), the political super-structure of accountability will have to change further. Economic convergence in stage two may take a long time before Britain matches German inflation and productivity rates. But when (and if) a single currency is reached, the sacrifice of economic sovereignty in loss of national control over exchange-rate and interest-rate policy will require a compensatory pooling of political sovereignty if EEC-wide financial and monetary measures are to be subject to any effective degree of political accountability.

That could take two different forms. In the weaker model the nation state structure as the dominant dimension of decision-making would be preserved, though with some limited extension of political control at the Euro-level. The central monetary authority would be responsible for achieving financial stability and combating inflation, but should also be required to take account of the need for balanced economic development and for securing high employment levels. For this purpose the Governor of the Euro-Fed central bank would be required to report both to ECOFIN (the Economic and Financial Council of Ministers) and to the Euro-Parliament economic/financial committee at reasonably frequent intervals (say, every three months) to be cross-examined on the balance of his policy, like the governor of the Federal Reserve before the US Congress. It would be necessary for budgetary policy to have the power to alleviate gross regional inequalities in order to promote balanced economic development, so the present scale of the EEC budget, at 1 per cent of GDP, would have to be increased some 5–8 fold.

Under the stronger model, a federal governmental structure would be required at least as far as central economic decisions are concerned, though still with maximum decentralisation of power on a range of other issues to either the nation state or regional levels. For only a major pooling of political sovereignty, it might be said, would be an adequate counter-weight to the economic power of the Euro-Fed.

This model would transform existing EEC institutions. The new Euro-Government would be directly elected throughout the EEC (indirect nominees from national parliaments would not command the same authority). The Commission would no longer have the prerogative of bringing forward legislation – that right would now belong to the Euro-government – and the Commission would shift to its natural role of civil service. The function of approving, or rejecting, legislative proposals would switch from the Council of Ministers, whose role would now be superseded, to a much revamped Euro-parliament with a range of new powers adequate to hold the federal government to account.

It is doubtful however whether the idea of a Euro-government with such overriding authority throughout the EEC would yet be acceptable to all its potential citizens. It would require its people to 'feel' more European – communautaire – than either British, French, German or whatever, and to accord their ultimate loyalties to the sense of being European. Despite the growing ties and the greater inter-mingling of peoples in recent decades, *that* degree of unified loyalties seems unlikely to be reached for a further few decades yet.

That will be even more the case if the EEC decides, as it should, to widen its coverage – to Sweden, Austria, the other Scandinavians and perhaps Hungary, Czechoslovakia and other East Europeans – before it deepens its integration. To that extent political unification, which must be organic and cannot be artificially generated, is out of kilter with some over-optimistic schedules for economic and monetary union. Because any attempt to force one without the other would break down, it seems clear that longer timetables will be needed before Europe, rather than the current nation states, is widely and naturally seen as the source of democracy and political accountability. For the overriding criterion will be that the peoples of Europe will only accept the new structures, whatever the visions of politicians or the dictates of the economic agenda, if they are satisfied that they will enhance their power to shape events and to gain greater control over their lives.

14

Power for What?
The Purpose of People

The central themes of this book have been that the spread of power and opportunity that is now centralised in few hands should be widened to the broad mass of the people; that people should be empowered to take control of their own lives; that a creative and participative society should be genuinely opened up for all citizens, not just a privileged few. Yet that should not be the sole theme, or even the main theme, of the radical left. Empowerment within the market is one thing. But people are far far greater than the market or any other economic system that may be devised. It is the economy that should serve people, not people the economy. The real argument against privatised market capitalism is that it reduces people to a flat single-dimension de-humanised existence. It completely fails to embrace, let alone understand, the rounded creativity of human beings.

Transcending the Market

There are two major reasons why the capitalist dream of universal materialism will not work. One is that the single-minded pursuit of wealth will founder both on the lack of availability of basic resources if materialism is to be world wide, and also on the incapacity of the environment to cope with the degree of interference implied, as Chapter 3 showed. The other reason is that it represents such a hugely lop-sided view of the fundamental nature of the human condition as to be profoundly unsatisfying and one that is self-destructive in the long run.

People are not in any sense primarily economic beings. Their social needs, cultural interests, artistic and aesthetic heritage, and spiritual aspirations are each just as important and together are certainly more central to their existence. An undiluted philosophy of enrichissez-vous very quickly begs the question of what is it all *for*, and at what price it is bought? None of this is of course to suggest that economic efficiency and competitiveness are not necessary. It is rather that they need to be integrated with other goals, and there can be no doubt that they were exaggerated out of all proportion in Thatcherite Britain.

No political philosophy can fully satisfy unless it seeks to answer the deepest questions about the purpose and meaning of human existence. No philosophy of the marketplace even engages this dimension. The totem of gross national product (GNP) cannot begin to embrace qualitative goals such as democracy, freedom, human dignity, self-realisation or personal fulfilment. It does not even achieve qualitative distinctions within the economic sphere so as to identify growth that is pathological, unhealthy, disruptive or destructive. It provides no measure of such crucial indices of the state of national feeling as frustration, alienation, insecurity or congestion.

GNP takes no account of the fact that materialism, which it does measure, is so limiting. It denotes the amassing of material wealth for the self which, while providing immediate gratification, ignores the deeper sources of human satisfaction in commitment to others, to the community and to external causes. As was said a long time ago and it remains no less true today, a man can gain the whole world and lose his own soul, and it profits him nothing. There has never been a truer epitaph of the shallowness of capitalism.

There is no more tyrannical or deadening a judgement than that such-and-such a proposal is 'uneconomic'. An activity may be economic though it plays havoc with the environment or with social needs, yet a competing activity, even if at some cost it protects and conserves the environment or advances personal or social happiness, is ruled out of court as uneconomic. The market is indeed the institutionalisation, not merely of individualism, but of irresponsibility.

The dynamism of the socialist ethic, by contrast, stems from the belief that people are the measure of the highest value in society. The fundamental criticism of capitalism is not its wastefulness nor even its failure to provide adequate welfare, but the fact that it impairs the wholeness of a person's personality. It treats labour as a commodity in a commodity market. As a result work is treated as a function which has little or no relation to the personal life and self-expression of the worker.

The Supremacy of Human Values Beyond the Self

In the end, by pursuing their own interests to the limit, as capitalism exhorts them to do, people will never find happiness. The essence of human aspirations cannot be reduced to self-grati-fication. It is rather to *values* and ideals which extend far above and beyond the self. Any political philosophy that fails to recognise that diminishes people and cannot provide long-term the deep inherent satisfaction that is the sole source of real happiness.

It is unfashionable to talk of values, especially spiritual values, because it conflicts with the dominant ethic of the twentieth century, scientific materialism, which is striving precisely to be value-less. Yet it is surely the fundamental flaw of our modern value-arid society that, this century, all the prevalent concepts of people have sought, and failed, to explain the human condition in terms of some lower order code, as though man's unique comprehending of values did not exist.

Marxism interpreted religion, philosophy, art and culture as disguised economic interests. Darwinian evolution stressed the development of higher forms from lower and competition via natural selection to bring about the survival of the fittest. Freud reduced human will to the sub-conscious conflicts of the mind. Relativism has been a force to deny all absolutes, norms and standards. Positivism as a movement has renounced all knowledge other than that obtained through the techniques of the natural sciences. And now Hayek, and his disciple Thatcher, have subordinated all man's strivings to the economic imperative of the market. What all these have in common, besides their grandiose claim to hold the explanation for all human phenomena, is their basic premise that any concept of higher-order being is reducible by a process of semi-mathematical logic to a lower one.

Such systematic reductionism not only generates total despair by denying any purpose or meaning to human life on earth, it is profoundly mistaken. There is nothing more basic to the understanding of the nature of the human condition than the recognition of the existence, and the uniqueness, of the human spirit. As philosophers from Aristotle to Schumacher have proclaimed, there is a metaphysical element to human nature, a higher order of being, that separates humans from all other creatures. It is that that theories of mankind as compliant to market disciplines, or any other creed of the psychological, physiological or economic reductionism of the human person, cannot begin to satisfy.

That unique aspect of human nature can only be fulfilled through a person's social ambitions of the highest order. He or she can only be at one with themselves at the deepest level if they are at one with those around them – neighbours, local community, fellow-citizens within their nation, and indeed at the international level, in terms of the kind of world in which they live. This is what has always inspired socialists to put their faith in the realisation of the brotherhood of man, in the impulse of altruism and sharing, and in the ideal of freedom for all through equal chances for all. It is what has always impelled the socialist conscience to cry out against poverty, the ugliness of deprivation, and the crime of stifled liberties and opportunities.

While therefore empowering people in the market or mixed economy should be a key part of the socialist credo, it is not by itself sufficient. *The use to which that power is put is just as important.* If it is used exclusively for self-aggrandisement or self-gratification, it is not a socialist empowerment. It is only socialist if that enhanced power is used creatively to benefit others or to contribute to a better community or environment. By a paradox unique to human nature, only then is it genuinely satisfying to the individual concerned.

A Socialist Vision of Society

How might this somewhat mystical vision of people be achieved in practical policy terms? There are effectively two choices facing us in planning the future of society. Britain could aim to become a super-industrial society dominated by big science, big technology, and large-scale knowledge and service industries. This would mean giving top priority to issues like nuclear power, automation, behavioural psychology, genetic engineering and biotechnology, and space colonisation. The goal would be super-growth, the use of science to stretch to the maximum existing energy limits, economic productivity limits, social, psychological and physiological limits, and indeed the ecological limits of the planet earth itself.

Such a scenario would however create a small technocratic elite and a large majority of second-class citizens in a permanently divided society. It would also at the international level create a small dominant group of hyper-industrialised countries and a mass of less developed countries in a permanently divided world. Such deep and abiding divisions are a classic recipe for enduring conflict.

The other central choice is for a post-industrial society which gives pride of place to people, to the quality of their lives, and to their scope for self-development. While the industrial revolution concentrated relentlessly on machine-driven, technology-driven, market-driven advance at enormous human cost, the post-industrial age would concentrate primarily on human growth. It would require a change of direction, rather than an acceleration, of today's main trends – towards greater self-sufficiency rather than even greater specialisation; towards greater self-reliance rather than ever greater dependence on big organisations and big technologies; towards de-centralisation rather than ever more centralisation; towards 'small is beautiful' rather than 'big is best'. This emphatically does not mean going back to pre-industrial conditions. But it does mean giving a different direction to what technology and scientific advance is *for*.

For industry and business we need a new set of guiding principles: selective growth that balances harmoniously with the environment, co-operation and participation to replace confrontation, and the scaling down of over-large, remote and over-complex organisations. Perhaps the most damaging consequence of current industrial and business structure is alienation – the feeling the worker has that he or she does not belong, has no say and no status, and is just a dehumanised digit in the machine. The answer to that is real employee involvement in the purpose as well as the performance of a job, not so much at remote boardroom level but primarily at shop-floor level. A major role for self-managing groups in factories and operating departments of business has to be found.

Equally the revolution in micro-processor computer-controlled automation and telecommunication systems should be put to use to improve the quality of living. It can free people from much drudgery and laborious work, though at the price of requiring extensive re-training of those made redundant. It can also offer a boon for de-centralising work opportunities, particularly for men or women with domestic responsibilities and for disabled persons. For people do not all have to work in one place when sub-units can be linked by data transmission systems. Indeed the world's first generation of tele-commuters is well under way. Moreover, a scatter of small self-managing units should be happier places to work in.

Similarly a new approach is desperately required to the future of our inner cities. The option of large-scale rural resettlement needs to be opened up, but for those who stay, a policy of 'villagisation' of the cities should be embarked upon, making them more humane and convivial places to live and work in, as well as economically viable. Whether it is small local businesses or co-operatives, community enterprises, self-help housing, small urban farms, neighbourhood action to create a new park or playground, or any other kind of personal or DIY initiative, we should be motivating a new generation of social entrepreneurs to undertake a multitude of such projects.

An entirely different focus is also needed for the running of our public services. The education system does not provide most people with a good preparation for life, for work, or for personal growth. The health service is really a sickness service, encouraging people to become dependent on treatment and drugs. The social services are chronically over-stretched partly because they themselves stimulate dependence. Experiments should be encouraged country-wide as to how to make schools, health centres, hospitals, social service offices and job centres into much more active centres of local community life.

This links in with new concepts of work. A vast amount of unpaid work of an essential kind – looking after the family at home and doing services for neighbours – has traditionally been done by women, while men went out to work at paid jobs. Men and women have now begun to share the two kinds of work (and the unemployment) more equally. This trend will, and should, continue. One result should be giving useful unpaid work as much esteem as paid work in a job. But that is not enough. Unemployed people, for example, who want to do unpaid voluntary work could be encouraged to do so without losing their unemployment benefit. More generally it requires that at least some currently unpaid work, without undermining proper family responsibilities and genuine philanthropic motives, should be remunerated. Patterns of family life would change and local communities would become more vital.

In pursuit of the crucial goal of full employment, available jobs could be shared around more widely not only by reducing overtime, but by increasing holidays, by giving sabbaticals, by work-sharing, by reducing the length of the working week and by instituting a flexible decade of retirement. Rural unemployment could be cut by a big increase in small, often part-time farming and by developing small rural industry, especially by encouraging wider use of small-scale advanced technologies.

But environment-friendly technologies are not enough. Big changes should be made in energy policy to maximise conservation. Government should change the complacent mood about wasteful energy use by a few dramatic shocks. It could phase out the production of large petrol-greedy cars and trucks, and transfer freight from road to rail. It could strictly regulate space-heating maximum temperatures in all public buildings and large offices. It should slow down sharply the rate of extraction of North Sea oil and switch a major slice of budgeted expenditure from nuclear power to alternative energy sources, both solar, wind and wave. It should establish the concept of energy accounting, judging policies and products by their energy cost, with penal taxation or prohibition of some energy-expensive products or activities.

The Socialist Dynamic

A vision is one thing; a drive to make it reality another. Too often the left's vision has been couched in static terms, redolent with the language of 'rights', 'entitlements', 'minimum standards', 'security' or 'citizenship'. Of course all of these are important and necessary, but they are all essentially reactive. Either they conjure up the picture of passive recipients or they offer a protective floor or some limitation against the abuse of authority by the power-brokers of society.

For the same reason the imagery of the 1940s welfare state is now very dated. It oozes with the aura of paternalism, bureaucracy, dependency and a world of claimants. It emphasises the availability of rights and benefits, often perceived pejoratively as 'handouts', while neglecting the reciprocity of responsibilities, duties and obligations. However valued are the basic principles of a welfare society, an appeal to them can no longer by itself inspire victory at a general election, as Labour's experience in both 1987 and 1992 revealed.

If the left's ideology is to regain resonance and force, it must recapture the power to inspire. It must be, and be seen to be, a vision that releases new forces in society, unlocks individual and group energies now pent up, and unleashes hidden talents. Socialism is not merely, or even primarily, about protecting the weak. It is much more about extending widely throughout the population the can-do mentality which under Thatcherite capitalism was the exclusive preserve of an entrepreneurial elite.

Not least the new socialist ideology must generate excitement. Traditional socialism, while enormously worthy and full of good works, was also rather dull and stifling. A left vision that can sweep the country needs to develop a raw cutting edge. A genuine human politics cannot thrive purely on the cultivation of high ideals, let alone the suffocating demands of respectability; it must also arouse a crusading passion.

Putting real power into the hands of the powerless and making that new power a foundation for an enhanced contribution to one's country offers a dynamic infinitely more resilient and meaningful than the Thatcherite consumerism of share handouts and capital discounts unconnected to the actual levers of power. Such a vision, as it was steadily implemented, would proliferate new cadres for socialism with the same ardour that Thatcher spawned her shock troops on the ground, the purveyors of private capital in every niche and cranny of the economy.

It involves a project on a scale of mobilisation never previously attempted by any socialist movement anywhere, even in Sweden. It represents a reversal of traditional top–down social democratic planning. It would progressively unleash bursts of undreamt-of activity where decentralisation of power would force government painfully to adjust from the use of hierarchical controls to increasing acceptance of self-reliance and self-discipline. But as an agenda for the left, as a foundation for the drive to wrest political and ideological dominance from the renascent radical right in Britain and throughout Europe, the scope is awesome.

Index